# What others are sayi

*Why Can't I Get This Jesus ~~Thing Right?~~*

In *Why Can't I Get This Jesus Thing Right*, author Scott Schuler provides a guide for those who are struggling. Forged out of his passion to come alongside others in the trenches and seasoned with transparency, it's a weapon we need in our faith arsenal. The personal experiences are shared with humility to illustrate foundational biblical truth—pointing those who read it to the ultimate answer—Jesus Christ. It's a book we'll all return to again and again.

**~Edie Melson, Award-winning Author & Director of the Blue Ridge Mountains Christian Writers Conference**

"As a pastor for twenty-seven years, one of the most important numbers I focused on was eighteen … eighteen inches between the head and heart, marking the most difficult battleground for the souls of mankind. My experience reveals that too many Christians are practically orphaned after coming to faith, left to fend on their own with little-to-no-guidance of how to engage in this battle of eighteen inches in biblically faithful and practical ways. Scott Schuler's work serves as a clarion voice calling out to spiritual orphans, guiding them into the way of walking with Jesus. Filled with practical wisdom and engaging stories, *Why Can't I Get This Jesus Thing Right?* provides a wonderful resource for individuals, Christian organizations and local churches to intellectually and relationally engage the whole person in the process of discipleship."

**~Bill Finley Search-Raleigh Area Director and former church planting pastor**

That question. Seriously, who hasn't asked that question? Scott Schuler puts it right out there in *Why Can't I Get This Jesus Thing Right?* And he puts it out there with heart. With biblical scholarship. With encouragement. With compassion and warmth. Whether you're new in the faith or a long-time sojourner, you can find practical tools to help on the journey to finding the life-changing, purpose-filled answers to that question. I'll read this one (that one) again.

**~Rhonda Rhea, TV personality, award-winning humor columnist, author of 19 books**

"Doth our teaching and preaching and learning reflect tha red-hot passion of them who be on fire fer Skipper and his Sun? Or doth we offer luke-warm words ter cold hearts? This be tha message of *Why Can't I Get This Jesus Thing Right?* Thar be lots ah feller could say 'bout this book, but tha long and short of it be this: getting Jesus and getting him right from tha get go 'ill send a feller or lass sailing towards tha Sun in ways lubbers kin only dream of. This captain keeps ah copy of "Get Jesus Right" under his bunk. I'd advise ya ter do tha same. We all go down ter Davy Jones. Make it yer task ter really know tha one who 'ill lift ya up from tha watery grave when yer time comes."

**~Eddie Jones, Tha Pirate Preacher — author of T*ha Pirate Gospel: The Adventures and Tales of John Mark,* and other middle grade and YA nonfiction and novels.**

Scott is a passionate and knowledgeable teacher of the Bible. He has a heart to disciple new believers, equip mature believers, and help every person live the life Jesus created them to live.

**~Chris Hankins, Lead Pastor, The Point Church**

*Why Can't I Get This Jesus Thing Right?* provides essential tools to take complexities out of understanding the Bible and navigating our walk with Jesus. Using relatable analogies, illustrations, and charts to help his reader visualize concepts, Scott journeys alongside the reader to point out Satan's detours, explain how to respond to God's voice, and reveal steps necessary to embrace the life God designed us to enjoy. I've known Scott for years. He thinks in sequential order. The walk from chapter to chapter is like having a GPS to chart your spiritual journey to become a true follower of Jesus.

**~Michael Stewart, Licensed Professional Counselor, Licensed Addictions Counselor Church Pastor of Bible Fellowship Baptist Church**

# Why Can't I Get This Jesus Thing Right?

# Why Can't I Get This Jesus Thing Right?

## Scott Schuler

Bold Vision Books
PO Box 2011
Friendswood, Texas 77549

Published by Bold Vision Books, PO Box 2011, Friendswood, Texas 77549

www.boldvisionbooks.com

Cover Design by Amber Wiegand-Buckley

Interior design by kae Creative Solutions

Illustrations by Amber Wiegand-Buckley, Mpavlov, and Maryna Kriuchenko

Published in the United States of America.

# Dedication

Jesus, thank you. This is your book. Use it to restore and redeem the lives of others, as you've done for me, and to raise up your followers.

To those struggling to find relationship and purpose with Jesus, like I was 25 years ago. Out of the transforming work of Jesus, I've written this book as your GPS. To grow in your own journey, turn the page.

And to my wife, Lory. Partner. Best friend. Your journey as a student of my teachings helped craft the voice for the reader. Without you, this book would not exist.

# Table of Contents

# Introduction

Life looked great. I was married. I had a prominent career, spacious home, active church leadership position, supportive friendships, and a secure future. But I was a puzzle with a missing piece.

I remember the day I committed to Jesus. I believed the message of the Gospel—he came to earth to pay my sin debt and rescue me. I also remembered the optimism and joy that filled me. I thought I could move a mountain with my bare hands. But now monumental challenges filled the valley before me. I was powerless. I wanted to do what the Bible said, yet lust and greed haunted me. The repetition became a cycle of frustration. Constantly seeking the next big thing— better job, more money, more fulfilling marriage and never being satisfied—left me exhausted and disenchanted. I wanted everything else more than I wanted Jesus.

*Why couldn't I get this following Jesus thing right?* I asked my trusted friends if they had experienced frustration too. Each one gave me a mixture of puzzled looks and counsel, "get more involved in church, read the Bible, pray, and serve, serve, serve!"

So I did.

My frustration amplified. I learned more about Jesus, the Bible, and meeting the needs of others, but I didn't connect to him. My cycle of frustration, wanting more mixed with the shame of dissatisfaction, whirled into a storm of guilt. It seemed I was a failure, and I couldn't be enough. *It was just too hard!*

One day, a faint image of Satan, the Enemy of every Christian, formed in my mind. He was standing off to the side, offering me a white towel to toss in as a sign of giving up on the Christian life.

Maybe you've experienced a similar cycle of frustration. You assumed you'd be further along the path on your journey with Jesus, no longer struggling with the same sin patterns—the behaviors, actions, and beliefs contrary to God's Word and truth (1 John 3:3, 5-6). You thought everything you've worked to achieve would bring happiness. Instead, you look for more—more answers and peace beyond human explanation. We've read about it—the abundant life of joy, hope, strength, and love of Jesus—but we cannot grab hold of it.

This battle is spiritual warfare. I determined to figure out what the Bible says about these unseen battles and how to overcome my sin patterns.

As I wrestled with those thoughts, I sensed nuggets of truth were within my grasp when I read these two verses in the book of Matthew. Jesus said,

> "Enter by the narrow gate. For the gate is wide and the
> way is easy that leads to destruction, and those who
> enter by it are many. For the gate is narrow and the way
> is hard that leads to life, and those who find it are few"
> (Matthew 7:13–14).

"Wait. Jesus," I said aloud, as if he were sitting across the table from me. "You say *life* in this verse. I thought *life* meant salvation. But do you mean there's more? Are you talking about experiencing a fully satisfying, abundant life now?"

I dared to challenge Jesus, "Show me this life. I want a relationship with you that is encouraging and joyful."

At first, I felt remorse over the demanding tone of my voice, but I made a decision that changed my life forever. "Jesus, do what you need to do so I can experience this life with you."

That day on the couch over twenty years ago began a lifelong pursuit. I used the Bible to answer tough questions and connect biblical dots. God's Word became such a part of me on this journey that it's my default response and defense. Through this process, I understand my purpose is to teach others what God has taught me.

## How to Approach This Book

My dad often told me, "You get out of life what you put into it." His principle holds true with this book. Having spent years writing, teaching, and mentoring men and women in their walk with God, I know you can learn more concerning the Christian faith and how to walk with Jesus.

But when you take intentional steps toward Jesus, you will become rich in a faith that will transform your life.

We'll start with the fundamentals I wish someone had helped me understand earlier. At the end of each chapter, I've provided action steps that will

> ➤ guide you through enemy territory,
> ➤ equip you for spiritual warfare,
> ➤ facilitate your surrender to Jesus, and
> ➤ enable you to live in the present moment.

As our path through the book narrows, I'll give you the tools Jesus revealed so you can better understand who you are in him and the purpose for your existence.

Consider *Why Can't I Get This Jesus Thing Right* as a guidebook for your journey. Write in the margins, underline phrases, and refer to topics as Jesus charts your course. Draw close to him on the narrow path that leads to abundant life.

# PART ONE

# Understanding Your Journey

"Enter by the narrow gate. For the gate is wide and the way is easy that leads to destruction, and those who enter by it are many. For the gate is narrow and the way is hard that leads to life, and those who find it are few" (Matthew 7:13-14)

*Chapter One*

# Where Do I Go From Here?

Godly influences lead you to abundant life
on the narrow path.

Lory looked over the group of women she had been mentoring, humbled by what God was doing. These women gathered on Monday nights to learn from Lory and each other. They laughed, cried, and prayed together, sharing struggles, celebrating victories, and studying words of hope and encouragement found in the Bible.

Tonight, Lory had shared from her journal dating back to points in her darkest times. Not to dwell in the past, but to call out the evil that was a part of Lory's history. The pages now felt more like someone else's story.

> Last night, the violence escalated to a physical fight in our bedroom. When I ran over to dial 9-1-1, he lurched

from behind, grabbed the phone and slammed it back down on the table. I will never forget the anger in his eyes, his voice growling with rage, "If you ever tell anyone about this, I'll kill you."

I'm ashamed to write it on paper, but here it goes. My four children and I live in a home consumed with verbal, physical, and substance abuse. Our home is beautiful on the outside, but inside it's a prison filled with dark secrets. The prison guard is my husband, the children's father—the abuser. He forbids us to talk about it. Not even to each other.

I know I've made poor choices, leaving one abusive relationship for another—a marriage beginning with overindulgent spending and partying with friends, tainted with drugs and alcohol.

The cut on my eye has stopped bleeding this morning. My chest and arm are already bruising. Not sure how I'm going to explain it to the kids. But these marks are just the physical signs. How have I allowed my life to come to this? How can I protect myself and my children? God, are you punishing me for my choices?

I don't get it! Mom and Dad raised me to believe in the goodness and protection of a loving God. I believed God created me for a special purpose, with gifts and talents that he would use to help others. Now I can't help myself.


(Four weeks later)

This morning, I've hidden in the guest bedroom with the door locked. I've got my Bible with me. God. I need hope! Please show me something.

And you did on the first page I opened, "For I know the plans I have for you,' declares the LORD, 'plans to prosper you and not to harm you, plans to give you hope and a future. Then you will call on me and come and pray to me, and I will listen to you. You will seek me and find me when you seek me with all your heart. I will be found by you,' declares the LORD, 'and will bring you back from captivity'" (Jeremiah 29:11-14 NIV).

"Plans? Hope? Future?" These words feel like foreign concepts. But I know they're your words, Father. I read them over and over.

"'I will be found by you,' declares the LORD, 'and will bring you back from captivity.'" That's it - captivity! Father, I've been a captive and you've released me from the chains.

Like a trap that has sprung open, I feel an emotional release deep inside. I realize I'm still locked away in my prison home. But I don't feel alone. A warm, almost tangible presence has filled the room. "Jesus, that's you!"

I come to you on my knees and beg you to forgive the mess I've created. Please help me find the person I used to be. I want to live as the person you've created me to be and spend my life serving you and loving others!

Somehow I feel power and I see light -- like stepping out of a darkly wooded trail into a clearing. I'm ready to take a step. I know this path won't be easy. Please protect me so no one can touch that deep part of me that I've given to you today, Jesus.

Rather than allowing her past to define the significance of her life, Lory sought God. He has now used these experiences to prepare her to help others on their journey.

God offers each person the same personal relationship Lory discovered. A fulfilling, abundant life. What about you? Do you believe God desires to walk with you?

## Spiritual Journey

You take spiritual steps every day—deliberately or unintentionally—that culminate in what God calls faith. You don't have to be ultra-spiritual. Every person possesses some form of faith, from faith in the chair you sit in, to faith the sun will rise tomorrow. Even the atheist has faith there isn't a God. Faith is a manifestation of everything you believe, trust, and follow. Is your faith founded in religious doctrine, taught by a particular church, or based on moral maxims that validate and complete your life? Or is your faith leading you to Jesus, who said, "I am the way, and the truth, and the life. No one comes to the Father except through me." (John 14:6)?

The desire for meaning in your life drives your faith and stems from a sense of emptiness and void, which comes from deep within, as you search for dignity, value, worth, and purpose. These voids take on myriad forms—deep darkness caused by sin or failure, unworthy feelings caused by rejection, or fear that causes indecision.

Identifying voids requires authentic reflection of what motivates, terrifies, or excites you. Years ago, my desire for the next big thing left an insatiable appetite for more. Once you define your voids, they no longer stalemate your life. But your heart's desire to fill them remains. Your heart is the unique spiritual part of you created by God to make you different from every other person. It not only includes your personality, but also how you think, dream, and respond to circumstances.

## Journey on the Narrow Path

God defined the narrow path that he sets before you (Matthew 7:14)—one that leads you to answer life's deepest questions. In Matthew 11:28–30, Jesus invites you on this journey.

"Come to me, all who labor and are heavy laden, and I will give you rest. Take my yoke upon you, and learn from me, for I am gentle and lowly in heart, and you will find rest for your souls. For my yoke is easy, and my burden is light."

*Come to* Jesus. *Come* is an invitation and a directive. He wants you to take intentional steps toward a fulfilling relationship with him. Beginning this journey requires you believe who the Bible says Jesus is and what he can do within you because biblical "faith is the assurance of things hoped for, the conviction of things not seen" (Hebrews 11:1).

When you come to Jesus, you will encounter him in a personal way. When I asked Jesus to help me overcome sin and walk in a purposeful life, he showed me I first needed heart change. Lory discovered that even though Jesus didn't remove her from her immediate circumstances, he walked with her through difficult times. Learning from Jesus brings your life into harmony with his. He will instill rest and peace in your heart. But can you define true rest and peace? And what is their relationship to your purpose in life?

➤ *Rest* means to no longer struggle through life in your own strength—to loosen your grip, trust, and allow God to sustain you.

➤ *Peace* is an inner contentment, regardless of what is happening around you.

➤ *Purpose* is knowing and fulfilling God's intended reason for your existence.

Jesus desires to infuse your heart with rest and peace through a personal relationship with him. This relationship leads you to the center of God's will, through the guidance of the Holy Spirit, and allows you to discover the purpose for which God created you.

Your journey on the narrow path to abundant life depends on the answer to three questions:

➤ How well do you know God?
➤ How well do you understand the Enemy?
➤ How well do you know yourself?

Like traveling to a new destination without a GPS, finding your way through these questions without a spiritual compass can be confusing. Many Christians try to navigate their faith journey without one, lost in their struggle to overcome obstacles, answer difficult questions, and avoid dangerous detours. Burdened by this for years, I wrote this book as a GPS for your journey. I will be your guide.

To knowing and living out the purpose for your existence

To recognizing and overcoming the Enemy's schemes to destroy

From seeking God to transformation

One of my greatest joys is recognizing God uses every part of my life. He does not waste one tear, painful moment, or joy-filled epiphany when I am walking in his presence. I took my relationship with Jesus steps beyond my initial commitment by seeking him with all my heart. Jesus said *few* find this life. I look forward to coming alongside you on this journey.

## Take Action

**1.** If you could describe your relationship with God using five words, what would they be?

Now, describe the relationship you *desire* to have with God.

**2.** What do you think made you pick up this book and read the first chapter?

## Next Step on the Path

How have choices and sin patterns affected your life? Read Ecclesiastes 1:1–3 to gain insight into the next chapter.

## Chapter Two

# Why Do I Always Want More?

Worldly influences lead us to destruction
on the wide path.

L ory and I love our ten-year-old daughter's carefree approach to
life. She sings, dances, or bounces into a cartwheel—regardless
of where she is. But she has another side too. She is frequently
discontent. She pursues gymnastics, swimming, or slime-making,
along with little girl toys such as Barbie dolls, horse figurines, jewelry,
and stuffed animals.

None of them fill the void in her heart. I understand, because playing
the *more* game did not satisfy me either. Solomon understood the
quest, too.

King Solomon, the son of King David, was a learned scholar, a
shrewd trader, and a powerful king. He enjoyed enormous wealth

and widespread influence. God told Solomon, "I give you a wise and discerning mind, so that none like you has been before you and none like you shall arise after you" (1 Kings 3:12). Imagine being Solomon, filled with wisdom and understanding beyond measure, and breadth of mind like the sand on the seashore.

Solomon's reputation for wisdom captured the interest of the Queen of Sheba, so she paid him a visit to "test him with hard questions."

> "And when she [the queen of Sheba] came to Solomon,
> she told him all that was on her mind. And Solomon
> answered all her questions; there was nothing hidden
> from the king that he could not explain to her. And
> when the queen of Sheba had seen all the wisdom of
> Solomon, the house that he had built, the food of his
> table, the seating of his officials, and the attendance
> of his servants, their clothing, his cupbearers, and his
> burnt offerings that he offered at the house of the LORD,
> there was no more breath in her" (1 Kings 10:2b–5).

No person before or since Solomon was as gifted, wise, and wealthy as he. Solomon had everything a person could ever desire. Yet he squandered his gifts, eventually wrecking his own life and causing the eventual division of the nation of Israel. Frustrated and floundering, Solomon drew this conclusion about life:

> "'Meaningless! Meaningless!'
> says the Teacher.
> 'Utterly meaningless!
> Everything is meaningless.'
> What do people gain from all their labors
> at which they toil under the sun?"
> (Ecclesiastes 1:2–3 NIV)

Maybe you've asked similar questions: "Why am I here? What's the point?"

I have.

Jesus promised an abundant life: "I came that they may have life and have it abundantly" (John 10:10b). Jesus is not referring to an abundance of possessions, power, or prestige, as Solomon and I thought. What are we missing?

## A Wide Path of Worldly Influences

Nearly two thousand years ago, Jesus told a large crowd of people,

"For the gate is wide and the way is easy that leads to
destruction, and those who enter by it are many"
(Matthew 7:13).

Most will take the easy way. On this wide path of worldly influences, life seems to be full of choices. Believe the philosophy you like and follow the most convenient religion. The wide path is not limited to the free-spirit or the agnostic. The wide path entices believers, too. Solomon knew God well, yet he gravitated toward worldly influences.

Not so different from twenty-first-century Christians.

## Striving to Fill Your Heart Voids

Voids are like Swiss cheese. Some portions of our heart are solid and healthy, while other areas have holes carved out by pain, failure, broken trust, or life-altering incidents such as molestation, rape, or a loved one's death. These voids cause you to feel unfulfilled, angry, or unworthy. The void spaces fill up with doubt, fear, despair—or sin.

Some people avoid the word sin, thinking it is too harsh or judgmental. But the Bible uses this broad term to define any unintentional or deliberate act of disobedience against God. Sin results in separation or independence from God.

Some of us cope with our voids by identifying as a martyr, seeking pity and condolences from others. Some of us see ourselves as victims, so we build unhealthy heart boundaries to keep everyone out. Becoming a martyr is a form of self-importance or reverse-pride. And a victim builds walls for protection from pain, attempting to prevent love from entering our heart—mentally, emotionally, and even physically. As either a martyr or a victim, we may believe no one could fathom our turmoil, brokenness, pain, or loneliness. We feel isolated and entitled to our negative feelings.

Until we handle these mental, emotional, and physical voids appropriately—according to God's Word—they will continue to desensitize our hearts and drive us to seek fulfillment in something or someone else. Like a child who constantly wants more.

I was frequently discontent, wanting the "next big thing." I turned to hobbies, careers, and possessions to fill me. Eventually, I flipped to the minimalist approach. Instead of getting a new car every two to three years, I took great pride in holding on to an old clunker for ten plus years. But all my appetites were meaningless. Nothing brought me joy.

Examine yourself. How do you attempt to fill your heart voids?

> Gossip, anger, or jealousy?
> Material wealth and possessions?
> Compulsive eating, spending, gambling?
> Careers, relationships, sex outside of marriage?
> Drinking or drug use?

Did you know volunteering or serving at the expense of other priorities can be attempts to fill your heart voids?

Striving toward minimalism is another pursuit to fill the emptiness.

Regardless, our attempts will fail as completely as Solomon's did. We'll arrive at his conclusion: "Meaningless! Meaningless!" says the Teacher... "everything is meaningless" (Ecclesiastes 1:2 NIV).

God alone must remain the focus of your spiritual journey. In Ecclesiastes, Solomon says thirty-eight times that *all is vanity (meaningless)* in life. This form of repetition is an author's way of driving home a point. A man who possessed everything laments all is meaningless *under the sun*. What does Solomon mean by *under the sun?* He is referring to all the worldly influences and experiences one can encounter in this lifetime:

**Career and work.** "What do people gain from all their labors at which they toil under the sun?" (Ecclesiastes 1:3 NIV). Work is necessary. But are you prioritizing work over God and loved ones, robbing yourself of meaningful relationships?

**Ambitions and goals.** "Yet when I surveyed all that my hands had done and what I had toiled to achieve, everything was meaningless, a chasing after the wind; nothing was gained under the sun" (Ecclesiastes 2:11 NIV). My ambitions for success destroyed my previous marriage. What goals are driving you?

**Novelty and adventure.** "What has been will be again, what has been done will be done again; there is nothing new under the sun" (Ecclesiastes 1:9 NIV). Wise people learn from history. Are you choosing novelties of the world or adventures with an eternal focus?

**Justice and righteousness.** "Again I looked and saw all the oppression that was taking place under the sun: I saw the tears of the oppressed—and they have no comforter; power was on the side of their oppressors—and they have no comforter" (Ecclesiastes 4:1 NIV). Evil fills our world. Only God offers true justice and righteousness. Are you looking for redemption and freedom in broken people?

**Wealth and possessions.** "I have seen a grievous evil under the sun: wealth hoarded to the harm of its owners" (Ecclesiastes 5:13 NIV). Money isn't bad. But pursuit of possessions and status leads to greed and a false sense of control. "For the love of money is a root of all kinds of evils" (1 Timothy 6:10). What pursuits does your checking account reflect each month?

**Power and prestige.** "All this I saw, as I applied my mind to everything done under the sun. There is a time when a man lords it over others to his own hurt" (Ecclesiastes 8:9 NIV). Lording it over others means dominating through intimidation, positional leadership, or affluence. Jesus is God, but regarded others over himself, serving them first (Matthew 20:28). Do you have the mindset of Jesus or the attitude of entitlement?

**Knowledge and understanding.** "Then I saw all that God has done. No one can comprehend what goes on under the sun. Despite all their efforts to search it out, no one can discover its meaning. Even if the wise claim they know, they cannot really comprehend it" (Ecclesiastes 8:17 NIV). No matter how wise or well educated you are, you will never know everything about God's creation, life, death, and the hereafter. Do you maintain a humble, teachable spirit?

The bottom line: it is impossible to fill your heart voids with anything in this world. No matter how you search for meaning, the Enemy wins if your pursuit is not godly. The Enemy desires to lead you on the wide path to destruction, a wasted life. He knows that if he can convince you to fill your voids with what the world offers, he will control you and your destiny.

Imagine rush hour on a freeway. Cars filled with people zipping in and out of traffic, then changing lanes suddenly or slamming on brakes. Paying little heed to the safety of others. But this is a spiritual superhighway of worldly influences, people rushing to fill the voids. Drivers veer wildly toward one filler, then change direction or stop suddenly.

They don't understand how to reach the destination—how to fill the voids. Nor do they realize or care how their decisions affect others. Losing sight of their original goal, they run off the road, falling into a dark abyss. This wild, aimless spiritual highway leads to the destruction Jesus speaks of in Matthew 7:13—the ultimate ruin of an individual which is separation from God, forever.

## Solomon's Conclusion: A Profound Message to You

In the words of a man who had many regrets, Solomon ends Ecclesiastes frustrated and discouraged. He chooses the word *meaningless* once again to describe everything *under the sun.* Maybe Solomon realized he had wasted his life. He squandered the amazing gifts God had given him on pleasures and selfish gain.

"Now all has been heard;
here is the conclusion of the matter:
Fear God and keep his commandments,
for this is the duty of all mankind"
(Ecclesiastes 12:13 NIV).

With these words, Solomon offers sound advice.

## Fear God

Fear does not imply you should be afraid of God. Rather, develop awe and reverence for God as you grow to understand who he is. Fearing God generates a desire to worship, respect, and love him as you live in relationship with him. This right perspective of God removes human fearfulness and pain, replacing them with intimacy—or as I have seen it written, "in-to-me-see"—implying a relationship of transparency and mature faith.

## Keep His Commandments

Do what God tells you to do. God does not control you through a list of dos and don'ts. Instead, God reveals his path for you to walk in relationship with Jesus. On this path, God leads you with boundaries, wisdom, and direction, cautioning you to stay clear of the wide path.

Solomon concludes Ecclesiastes with a final warning: "For God will bring every deed into judgment, including every hidden thing, whether it is good or evil" (Ecclesiastes 12:14 NIV). Solomon yielded to the temptations that lured him away from God. His life, with all its riches, was unfulfilled. He lost focus of what was important because he took the bait of temptation offered so skillfully by the Enemy.

Our world today looks different from Solomon's world, but is there really anything new under the sun? No. Thousands of years after Solomon's death, his wisdom warns us that worldly influences take us down the wide path of destruction and separate us from Jesus. The only path to the abundant life Jesus offers is the one Solomon recommended: *Fear God. Keep his commandments.*

Just as a child needs time to grow into maturity, our spiritual journey requires time. Attempting to fill heart voids ourselves is a necessary part of our growth. The struggle helps us see what is important and how the world influences our commitment to Jesus. It may take many years for us to learn what is most important. But God keeps his promises. As we follow his instructions, he fills the voids in our heart.

## Take Action

**1.** Talk to God about your heart voids. Identify them here. What does he want you to do with them?

**2.** Do you find yourself on the wide path? Write out what you're doing wrong and where you think you'll end up.

## Next Step on the Path

Do you understand the connection between God, Jesus, and the Holy Spirit—and their connection to you? Read Ephesians 3:14–19 to gain insight into the next chapter.

# PART TWO

# Understanding Your God

"The grace of the Lord Jesus Christ and the love of God and the fellowship of the Holy Spirit be with you all" (2 Corinthians 13:14).

## Chapter Three

# How Can I Know All of God?

The Father, Son and Holy Spirit [the Trinity]
are central to every believer's experience.

For years I struggled to understand the Trinity—a word I had often heard in church. I believed all three persons—the Father, Son, and Holy Spirit—are God in One. Together, they are the Holy Trinity or Godhead.

But then I learned even though the Father is God, he is not the Holy Spirit or the Son. Jesus is God, but he is not the Father or the Holy Spirit. The Holy Spirit is God, too, but he is not the Father or the Son. What?

While I was on a trip to Ireland, a tour guide plucked a three-leaf clover from the field, turned it upside down, and pointed to the clover's three leaves. Each leaf represents a component of the Holy

Trinity—Father, Son, and Holy Spirit. Then, pointing to the stem, he explained three leaves on the clover are all-in-one on the stem.

Similarly, the Trinity operates with individually specific purposes, but the three are all-in-one as God. Because Jesus became fully human to pay the sin debt for humanity, he is the one with whom we walk in a personal relationship. The apostle Paul explains it this way in the New Testament:

> "There is one body and one Spirit, just as you were
> called to one hope when you were called; one Lord, one
> faith, one baptism; one God and Father of all, who is
> over all and through all and in all"
> (Ephesians 4:4–6 NIV).

It's confusing, I know. No matter your depth of Bible training, the individual roles of the Trinity can seem complex. Part of my job as your guide through this book is to simplify complicated concepts.

Let's use the job descriptions of a movie-production crew to help us understand.

Rather than a feature film lasting two hours, the time frame of God's story is eternity. The core plot is redemption—God's plan to ensure every person has the opportunity to go to heaven. God wrote the screenplay. The Father, Son, and Holy Spirit work together to write their story on your heart and to fulfill God's will for your life in his timing.

## The Director: God the Father

God is the creator and the author of his plan of redemption. He is the one who foretold this story long before human beings existed. He is both the visionary and the director.

In his story, God is redeeming mankind from the sin brought into his perfect creation through the enemy, Satan. Following the fall of Adam and Eve in Genesis 3:15, God put his plan of redemption into action, offering to rescue us from ourselves and from the sin that separated us from his presence and glory. Since this initial dark time in human history, God has been wooing us back to him through love and with promises.

As with most productions, the director's name appears prior to the first scene. The director's name gives the film credibility and tells viewers who had the financial clout to create the film. God, however, did not bankroll his story with money. The greatest love story ever written was financed in full through the blood of Jesus Christ—the main character.

## The Main Character: Jesus the Son

God's script—the sixty-six books of the Bible—clearly points people to Jesus, God's Son, as the main character. He is the Messiah, which means "the anointed one," the one sent to deliver mankind from the power of sin. Nothing illustrates this fact better than the 300 plus prophecies fulfilled through the life and death of Jesus. An online article from The Christian Broadcasting Network puts this into perspective:

> Mathematically speaking, the odds of anyone fulfilling this amount of prophecy are staggering. Mathematicians put it this way: 1 person fulfilling 8 prophecies: 1 in 1,000,000,000,000,000,000 1 person fulfilling 48 prophecies: 1 chance in 10 to the 157th power. 1 person fulfilling 300+ prophecies: Only Jesus![1]

[1] The Christian Broadcasting Network, Inc. https://www1.cbn.com/biblestudy/biblical-prophecies-fulfilled-by-jesus

Because people are oblivious to the biblical promises and prophecies regarding his birth, they do not see the truth in Jesus. They may know something is missing in their life, and they try to fill it rather than humbly seeking God. Throughout history, civilizations have created religions, truth, and methods of obtaining salvation.

Fear and insecurity, caused by human sinfulness, continue to drive our fevered pace to control our fate. God's story includes one story after another of faith and trust faltering and of darkness looming, as men and women turn against God time after time.

Yet in the darkness, we witness hope, laid out in great detail through the foretelling of Jesus, the Messiah, in the book of Isaiah, followed by the New Testament accounts of his life, death, and purpose in the four gospels—Matthew, Mark, Luke, and John. The book of Acts records the ascension of Jesus into heaven, and the apostle Paul's words (along with other New Testament writers) challenge all followers to walk with Jesus and encourage one another to experience the freedom found in Christ. Finally, in the book of Revelation, the Apostle John shares a foretelling of what is yet to transpire: the second coming of Jesus, who will redeem all those who believe in him.

Paul explained the significance of Jesus' second coming this way:

> "Therefore God has highly exalted him [Jesus] and bestowed on him [Jesus] the name that is above every name, so that at the name of Jesus every knee should bow, in heaven and on earth and under the earth, and every tongue confess that Jesus Christ is Lord, to the glory of God the Father" (Philippians 2:9–11).

God's story is a compelling production, with his Son, Jesus, playing the lead role and embodying truth and love. Without Jesus, there is no story—neither redemption from sin nor abundant life. Without Jesus, Christianity cannot satisfy the deep voids within every person.

The role of Jesus is the epicenter of the Christian faith and could not be fulfilled without the third and final component, the Holy Spirit:

> "The Helper, the Holy Spirit, whom the Father will
> send in my name, he will teach you all things and bring
> to your remembrance all that I have said to you"
> (John 14:26).

## The Producer: The Holy Spirit

A movie producer brings the entire production together. Similarly, the Holy Spirit carries the same divine power as God the Father, and his resurrected Son, Jesus Christ. At the risk of overgeneralizing the Holy Spirit's work, I will begin with this brief statement: The Holy Spirit is always working to draw people to Jesus the Son, the main character of God's story. The Holy Spirit resides in each follower at the moment of salvation; his role is to teach and encourage us how to walk with Jesus in relationship:

> "For the Spirit [Holy Spirit] searches everything, even
> the depths of God. For who knows a person's thoughts
> except the spirit of that person, which is in him? So also
> no one comprehends the thoughts of God except the
> Spirit of God. Now we have received not the spirit [the
> Enemy, Satan] of the world, but the Spirit [Holy Spirit]
> who is from God, that we might understand the things
> freely given us by God" (1 Corinthians 2:10a–12).

The work of the Holy Spirit is vast yet personal. Mysterious and sometimes quiet, but convicting and always cultivating.

The Holy Spirit takes up spiritual residence within us at salvation, but that does not mean we automatically are free from our frustrations and sinful patterns. The sanctifying work of the Holy Spirit is a lifelong process as we become less of our self and more of Jesus (John 3:30). We are set apart and freed from sin through sanctification, the constant work of the Holy Spirit, the producer.

## How Do God, Jesus, and the Holy Spirit Work Together?

The three persons of the Trinity work in unison to get your heart right with the Father, to deepen your personal relationship with the Son, and to learn through revelations of the Holy Spirit. In Ephesians 3, the apostle Paul shares a glimpse of how the Holy Spirit reveals the Father and Son to each Christian:

> "For this reason I bow my knees before the Father, from whom every family in heaven and on earth is named, that according to the riches of his glory he may grant you to be strengthened with power through his Spirit in your inner being, so that Christ [Jesus] may dwell in your hearts through faith—that you, being rooted and grounded in love, may have strength to comprehend with all the saints [followers] what is the breadth and length and height and depth, and to know the love of Christ that surpasses knowledge, that you may be filled with all the fullness of God" (Ephesians 3:14–19).

Although God, Jesus, and the Holy Spirit are all powerful and all knowing, they do not use their power to force anyone into relationship with them. Rather, they allow you to choose to have a relationship and to decide the depth of the relationship.

God the Father desires you choose him and the love of Jesus. He pursues you in love so you may know his forgiveness, his abundance, and be prepared for the role God has for you in the greatest story ever told.

I've learned to recognize the Holy Spirit at work, and he has helped me see the Father and the Son more clearly.

Imagine the three-leaf clover again. See how each one works in your life.

God
pursues you
and points
you to His
Son, Jesus

The Holy Spirit works
to sanctify you and
point others to the
Father and Jesus

Jesus walks
with you
and gives
you the
gifts of the
Holy Spirit

Just as the director, cast, and producer in a movie work together to create a blockbuster film, the Father, Son, and Holy Spirit are creating a masterpiece—you. The more you understand about their roles, the greater you will appreciate them.

## Take Action

**1.** Write about the connection between God the Father, Jesus the Son, and the Holy Spirit. How can this new understanding help you in your walk with Jesus now?

**2.** Journal one takeaway about the importance of Jesus' life and death fulfilling hundreds of prophecies and promises.

## Next Step on the Path

What would you say if someone asked you who Jesus is? Read Colossians 1:15–20 to gain a better understanding of how to answer the question.

*Chapter Four*

# Where Does Jesus Fit In?

**The mysterious depths of Jesus reveal he is the Christ, our Lord and Savior.**

Our Alaskan tour helicopter landed on a glacier. As I stepped out of the chopper, I understood the necessity of my spiked shoes, now preventing me from slipping on the slick ice. Gradually, my eyes adjusted to the light reflecting off the glistening white surface. That's when I saw the colors. Brilliant blues and deep purples bursting from the layers of ice beneath my feet. I was awestruck by colors I'd never seen before.

In a moment of worship I whispered, *Jesus, this is how you reveal the depths of your love and beauty to us, one extraordinary layer at a time.*

The well-known facts about Jesus are like the top layer of ice on the glacier. The foundational truths of his existence, such as his birth to the young virgin Mary. Living a sinless life. And his identity as the Son of God-crucified, obedient to death on a cross, and resurrected to eternal life. But until we get to the colorful depths of who Jesus is, we base our relationship with him on surface knowledge.

The Apostle Paul helps us understand the layers of Jesus' identity. "That Christ may dwell in your hearts through faith—that you, being rooted and grounded in love, may have strength to comprehend with all the saints [believers] what is the breadth and length and height and depth, and to know the love of Christ that surpasses knowledge, that you may be filled with all the fullness of God" (Ephesians 3:17-19).

To know Jesus is to know God. And only through salvation in Jesus can we live eternal life with God. That's why knowing the attributes of Jesus is foundational to us as followers. God fulfills his promises through his son, Jesus. And these are the promises we can stand on in good or bad times.

To simplify his identity, we will first establish the qualities that make Jesus unique. Then we'll look at the eternal promises he vows to every believer, as we become fully surrendered to him. These attributes and promises become part of how Jesus loves and ministers to us.

## The Unique Attributes of Jesus

Each of us has characteristics that make us different from every other individual. Jesus' existence as a person is superior and perfect. Although Jesus dealt with every challenge you will face, he never sinned.

**Jesus is** *the image of the invisible God.* In Colossians, Paul points to a fundamental truth about Jesus: he became wholly man; he was still wholly God.

> "He [Jesus] is the image of the invisible God, the first-
> born of all creation. For by him all things were created,
> in heaven and on earth, visible and invisible, whether

thrones or dominions or rulers or authorities—all things
were created through him and for him. And he is before
all things, and in him all things hold together"
(Colossians 1:15–17).

God, who is *invisible* because he is Spirit, is vividly portrayed in
the flesh by Jesus. As you read the biblical accounts of Jesus' thirty-
three years on earth, you will identify with him as a fellow human
being—filled with desires, dreams, and temptations. Yet he lived in
full accordance and obedience to God's Word.

Some people believe Jesus was a good and wise prophet, but they
struggle to accept him as God. In his commentary on *Galatians–
Colossians*, author Max Anders writes:

> Jesus is the image of God. The word for *image* was
> used in Paul's time for likenesses placed on coins,
> portraits, and for statues. It carries the idea of cor-
> respondence to the original… Hebrews 1:3 tells us
> that the Son is the radiance of God's glory and the
> exact representation of his being.[2]

**Jesus is** *the Christ, the Son of the Living God. Christ,* although
frequently connected with the name Jesus, is not Jesus' last name.
"*Christ,* comes from *Christos,* a Greek word meaning 'the anointed
one,' or 'the chosen one.' The Hebrew nation referred to Christ as
the *Messiah,* which means promised deliverer. In John 11:27 Martha,
sister of Lazarus, affirmed she believed in Jesus' deity, "Yes, Lord; I
believe that you are the Christ, the son of God, who is coming into
the world." Jesus allowed her to witness his resurrection power when
he raised Lazarus from the dead.

---

[2] Anders, M. *Galatians-Colossians*, Vol. 8 (Nashville, TN: Broadman & Holman Publish-
ers, 1999), 283.

The name Jesus Christ means Jesus, the Messiah—our Savior. The name Jesus Christ proclaims his divinity and affirms he is God.

**Jesus** *created all things.* Jesus did not come into existence when he was born (Matthew 1:23). Jesus was with God from before the beginning.

> "In the beginning was the Word [Jesus], and the Word [Jesus] was with God, and the Word [Jesus] was God. He [Jesus] was in the beginning with God. All things were made through him [Jesus], and without him [Jesus] was not any thing made that was made"
> (John 1:1–3).

Jesus is one with our Father God, but Jesus also came to live among humans on earth, and he modeled perfect holiness, sovereignty, supremacy, and love. He is in control of his creation. He prevents evil from prevailing and protects this world from falling into complete disorder. Jesus is the glue of the same creation to which you awaken every morning: *in him [Jesus] all things hold together* (Colossians 1:17a).

**Jesus is** *the head of the church.* Those who gather as followers in Christ comprise the Christian Church. As a group and individually, these followers seek a life made complete through faith in, obedience to, and relationship with Jesus. The first-century church described the church like a body and recognized Jesus' rightful position as *head of the church* as they gathered to learn more about Jesus and to worship him.

> "And he [Jesus] is the head of the body, the church. He [Jesus] is the beginning, the firstborn from the dead, that in everything he might be preeminent. For in him [Jesus] all the fullness of God was pleased to dwell, and

through him [Jesus] to reconcile to himself all things,
whether on earth or in heaven, making peace by the
blood of his cross" (Colossians 1:18–20).

What does it mean for Jesus to be the *head* of the church body? A local gathering of followers, a church, should be built on the foundation the Bible is the infallible truth, including the belief Jesus is God. The people in that church prayerfully rely on the Holy Spirit for direction and passionately lead others to Jesus and salvation in him.

This kind of church has appointed Jesus *as head over all things.* Its members worship Jesus by embracing and serving each other and by joyfully worshiping and growing together in Christ. Their primary goal is to glorify him and build his kingdom.

**When Jesus is not the head of the church—a word of caution.** Various denominations, or branches, exist around the world. No matter what the denomination is, however, when a *church* functions according to God's will and Word, Jesus—not a human being—is the leader of the church. According to the Bible, the church body is to reflect Jesus and to submit to his leadership.

There are telltale signs when a church has not established Jesus as its head:

➤ The church body worships its leaders instead of Jesus.
➤ Selfish gain, rather than glorifying Jesus, motivates the church's finances, ministries and programs.
➤ Leadership encourages a culture of serving over a relationship with Jesus. Although serving others is good, it cannot prevail over discipleship and seeking a personal walk with Jesus. Jesus came to serve, but his priority was time talking with his Father, as we witness numerous times in the New Testament.

➤ Pastoral messages temper basic tenets of scripture because these truths are too hard for the congregation to hear: 1) the only way to salvation and eternity with God is the narrow path with Jesus and 2) the Enemy is real and exists to cause evil in this world.

Jesus warned against such misapplication of biblical leadership when he prophesied to the seven churches in the first three chapters of the book of Revelation. While he recognized each church for their good and faithful works, he also exposed their sinfulness.

The Book of Revelation reveals the words of Jesus, who spoke to John through prophetic visions. Jesus reprimands the church in Laodicea, "I know your works: you are neither cold nor hot. Would that you were either cold or hot! So, because you are lukewarm, and neither hot nor cold, I will spit you out of my mouth. For you say, I am rich, I have prospered, and I need nothing, not realizing that you are wretched, pitiable, poor, blind, and naked" (Revelation 3:15–17).

Jesus uses the term lukewarm to describe a slow fade. There are churches today who, like the seven churches, abandon their vigorous pursuit of God's Word for a passionless attitude toward faith, prayer and discipleship. Their lukewarmness results from self-reliance and affluence, rather than dependence on God's provision. Complacency and permissiveness replace foundational truth, as they adopt culturally accepted norms into their beliefs.

When the foundation of a church is anything other than God's design—the attributes of Jesus—it will fail. In Matthew 16:18, Jesus said, "And I tell you, you are Peter, and on this rock I will build my church, and the gates of hell shall not prevail against it."

## The Everlasting Promises of Jesus

Lory and I work to teach our children how to be responsible, generous, loving people. We want them to develop godly characteristics that point others to Jesus. This is important because we love Jesus. And because we've learned the hard way how easy it is to hurt others. To feel unloved and unforgiveable. To lose our way and give up the fight. And no matter how well intentioned we are, we will break a promise from time to time.

But Jesus cannot break a promise. He cannot lie, and he will always follow through on what he said—in his time and according to his Father's will. Knowing the promises of Jesus is essential in our walk with him. From his promises stem our identity and confidence as believers.

**Love.** Jesus loves you unconditionally and eternally. (John 15:9)

**Identity.** You are a member of his royal family. (1 John 3:1)

**Presence.** Jesus is always with you. (Deuteronomy 31:8)

**Goodness.** Jesus lavishes you with his goodness, according to his plan. (Romans 8:28)

**Provision.** You will receive exactly what you need in his time. (Philippians 4:19)

**Protection.** Jesus protects you through his encouragement and support. (Psalm 54:4)

**Physical Sustenance.** Jesus equips your body to live out his purpose. (Job 33:4)

**Power.** The resurrection power of Jesus lives inside you. (Luke 1:37)

**Wisdom.** He provides divine understanding and clarity. (James 1:5)

**Tenacity and Perseverance.** You develop a patient determination to persevere. (Isaiah 40:31)

**Strength in Weakness.** His strength is perfected in your weakness. (2 Corinthians 12:9)

**Spiritual Armor.** Jesus covers you in his spiritual armor to stand firm against evil. (Ephesians 6:10-18)

**Unpredictability.** Jesus can move in you suddenly and when you least expect it, keeping you on the edge of your spiritual seat. (Isaiah 43:19)

**Leadership.** You will triumph in your battles by mirroring his attributes to others. (2 Corinthians 2:14)

**Listening Ear.** Jesus wants to hear from you. He listens with love and sympathy. (Psalm 145:18)

**Voice.** Jesus speaks to you in awesome and mysterious ways. (John 10:27)

## The Attributes and Promises of Jesus Are Sealed by God

Jesus purchased your salvation by dying on the cross in your place. Although life offers few guarantees, God put his *seal on* you, which refers to a mark of ownership, with a guarantee. "For all the promises of God find their Yes in him. That is why it is through him that we utter our Amen to God for his glory. And it is God who establishes us with you in Christ, and has anointed us, and who has also put his seal on us and given us his Spirit in our hearts as a guarantee" (2 Corinthians 1:20–22). God has given us his Spirit in our hearts. The Spirit connection guides us to the promises of Jesus.

Study the promises of Jesus. Put them on an index card and refer to them often for encouragement and strength. Like my experience on the Alaskan glacier, you may not see God's magnificent beauty and divine creativity at first. But the Holy Spirit will reveal the depths of Jesus as you relate to him as both man and God.

## Take Action

**1.** Read the list of Jesus' unique attributes and promises. Which one best describes how you see him and why?

**2.** Journal which of the promises is most important to you and why.

## Next Step on the Path

What makes the cross so significant in your faith as a Christian?
Read 1 Corinthians 15:1–4 and write what Jesus is saying.

## Chapter Five

# Why Is the Cross a Big Deal?

God's plan of man's redemption and eternal life is only possible through Jesus' sacrifice on the cross.

Soldiers nailed his hands and feet to the cross with five- to seven-inch iron spikes. With the first blow, the spikes pierced the outer layer of skin and flesh. With each successive blow, the spikes ripped through the muscle tissue, blood vessels, veins, and nerve endings. They penetrated the back of his hands and the bottom of his feet, pinning him to the splintered wooden cross. We can only imagine the physical pain.

Prior to his crucifixion, Jesus was brutally flogged and scourged for crimes he had not committed. He was beaten with a short whip, likely bearing balls of lead or sharp objects at the end of each leather strip. The blows from the whip, coupled with the force from the weighted objects, would have shredded Jesus' skin and eventually cut into his tissue, tearing the muscles from his shoulders, back, and legs.

Roman soldiers then forced Jesus to carry his cross. The trek would have been difficult for any man, but it was excruciating for someone whose back had endured such barbaric abuse. With an estimated weight of more than 150 pounds, he dragged the cross to the place where his life would end. It's hard to believe Jesus' tragic death was God's plan for his Son. But it would be harder to grasp a world in which God did not have a plan to save us from our sin.

## The Necessity of a Plan

When I was in my late teens, I built a small addition on the side of our family home. I believed I was savvy enough to build this addition without a blueprint. So I gathered materials and tools and set to work. After laboring for several weeks, I was pleased as I stepped back to admire my masterpiece. I had no idea it would soon be an expensive lesson in humility.

It was late into my double shift at work when Mom called, "Scott, the new building is flooding with rain." Anxiety swept through me as I sped home to find water engulfing the room. Four inches of water covered the floor. Timbers were already leaning and wall finishes were peeling away.

> "And the rain fell, and the floods came, and the winds
> blew and beat against that house, and it fell, and great
> was the fall of it" (Matthew 7:27).

I dug trenches, alternating between a shovel and my bare hands, desperately trying to drain the water away from the addition. But it was too late. Hours later the foundation crumbled apart, the roof started sagging, eventually tearing away completely. A mixture of rain, sweat, and tears ran down my face, as I stared at the colossal failure.

How often can we trace our failures back to poor foundational values or plans. Because God knows our inclination toward poor choices, he established Jesus as the cornerstone of our faith. Jesus' life, death and resurrection were God's plan from the beginning.

## Jesus Was and Is the Plan

Although he knew the cost, Jesus willingly stepped into God's plan for his life.

> "And the Word [Jesus] became flesh and dwelt among
> us, and we have seen his glory, glory as of the only Son
> [Jesus] from the Father [God], full of grace and truth"
> (John 1:14).

The Apostle John proclaims Jesus as the *Word*, which seems hard for us to understand. The Greek word translated *Word* is *logos,* meaning "reason" or "plan." Jesus is the *Word* of God in the flesh. The Word is God's way of communicating with us. The Word is alive, active and powerful (Hebrews 4:12). God spoke the world into existence (Genesis 1:1-25). God spoke and created man (Genesis 1:25-27). And nothing speaks more clearly of God's love for mankind than his plan for Jesus on the cross.

> "But it was the LORD's [God the Father's]
> good plan to crush him [Jesus] and cause him grief.
> Yet when his [Jesus'] life is made an offering for sin,
> he [Jesus] will have many descendants.
> He [Jesus] will enjoy a long life, and the LORD's
> good plan will prosper in his [Jesus'] hands"
> (Isaiah 53:10 NLT).

God's plan for the redemption of our sins, through the blood sacrifice of his Son, is outlined in Isaiah's prophecy. A prophet is a person who speaks the words of God [prophecy] to bring correction and encouragement in a specific circumstance or in a future unspecified time. But Isaiah wrote his words more than seven hundred years prior to the birth of Jesus Christ. Through Isaiah, God shared his miraculous plan, fulfilled in God's timing—when Jesus came to earth.

## The Plan: Fully Human, Fully God

The Father sent his son Jesus into the world to die. His sacrifice helps us realize how heartbreaking the plan must have been to God. Yet he loved us so much (John 3:16) that he sacrificed his son for us.

> "Who has believed our message? To whom has the LORD [God the Father] revealed his powerful arm? My servant [Jesus] grew up in the LORD's [God the Father] presence like a tender green shoot, like a root in dry ground. There was nothing beautiful or majestic about his [Jesus'] appearance, nothing to attract us to him. He [Jesus] was despised and rejected—a man of sorrows, acquainted with deepest grief. We turned our backs on him [Jesus] and looked the other way. He [Jesus] was despised, and we did not care" (Isaiah 53:1–3 NLT)

Jesus gave up everything in heaven to live on earth, as an example of God's perfect love. Jesus "emptied himself" and "humbled himself," as described in Philippians 2:5–8: "Have this mind among yourselves, which is yours in Christ Jesus, who, though he was in the form of God, did not count equality with God a thing to be grasped, but emptied himself, by taking the form of a servant, being born in the likeness of men. And being found in human form, he humbled himself by becoming obedient to the point of death, even death on a cross."

By surrendering his heavenly rights, Jesus *emptied himself* to live as a *servant* on earth—fully human and fully God. He did not give up his divinity or his heavenly spiritual powers. But he was submissive to his Father's guidance (John 5:19), demonstrating perfect obedience and discipleship.

## The Plan: Wrongfully Accused

Jesus stood before the religious leaders and people of Israel and declared, "I am the way, and the truth, and life. No one comes to the Father except through Me" (John 14:6). Many refused to believe him. But Jesus simultaneously demonstrated purity and holiness as he exercised his powers of healing, deliverance, and prophecy, and he exposed the heresy of the religious leaders. Jesus turned the religious traditions set forth in the Mosaic law (the laws God gave Moses) upside down. Caught up in their religiosity, the leaders vowed to get rid of Jesus. Convinced he was only a man, not the Messiah sent by God to redeem them.

When Jesus declared he was God, the religious leaders considered his claims blasphemy. According to the Mosaic law, blasphemy was speaking sacrilegiously about God or sacred things and punishable by death. The crime of blasphemy included comparing oneself to God and demeaning his authoritative omniscience.

When sentenced to death, the religious leaders thought they were also destroying his message of eternal life. But God was fulfilling his plan—*to seek and to save the lost* (Luke 19:10).

Isaiah described Jesus' trial and crucifixion even though it was hundreds of years before it happened.

"He [Jesus] was oppressed and treated harshly, yet he [Jesus] never said a word. He [Jesus] was led like a lamb to the slaughter. And as a sheep is silent before the shearers, He [Jesus] did not open his mouth. Unjustly condemned, he [Jesus] was led away. No one cared that he died without descendants, that his [Jesus'] life was cut short in midstream. But he [Jesus] was struck down for the rebellion of my people. He [Jesus] had done no wrong and had never deceived anyone. But he [Jesus] was buried like a criminal; he [Jesus] was put in a rich man's grave" (Isaiah 53:7–9 NLT)

## The Plan: Fear and Pain

Jesus is God; therefore, some people assume he easily handled the suffering inflicted on him. But because of his humanity, Jesus struggled with emotional and physical pain, just as we do. He endured all the abuse without succumbing to sinful thoughts, words, or actions. Isaiah said,

"Yet it was our weaknesses he [Jesus] carried; it was our sorrows that weighed him [Jesus] down. And we thought his [Jesus'] troubles were a punishment from God, a punishment for his [Jesus'] own sins!" (Isaiah 53:4 NLT).

Prior to his arrest and crucifixion, Jesus and the disciples spent time in the Garden of Gethsemane. Matthew paints a clear picture of the anguish Jesus suffered and expressed to his Father. Jesus was human and felt pain as he anticipated his execution:

"Then he [Jesus] said to them [twelve disciples], 'My soul is very sorrowful, even to death; remain here, and watch with me.' And going a little farther he fell on his face and prayed, saying, 'My Father, if it be possible, let this cup pass from me; nevertheless, not as I will, but as you will'" (Matthew 26:38–39).

Jesus endured two kinds of suffering: the mental anguish of the impending agony of the cross *as a man* and the burden of becoming the ultimate sacrifice—paying the price for the sins of the world *as God*. That suffering was the *cup* to which he referred. Jesus also experienced rejection: Jewish religious leaders accused and condemned him; Roman leaders persecuted him; the twelve disciples abandoned him.

Jesus did not hide behind false humility; neither did he hide his feelings. He revealed his heart and anguish to his Father. In doing so, Jesus showed it is okay to express our feelings to God.

Years ago, struggling with wanting my life to be perfect, I knew that my marriage was not. I was angry at God. Frustrated, I decided to take a lone walk on the beach and throw an adult tantrum. Like a balloon about to burst, angry words left my lips. I knew immediately I'd crossed the line. I cried out in remorse and asked God to forgive me. Thankfully, God is merciful. The peace he gave me allowed me to surrender my marriage to him that evening. Although we divorced years later, God walked with me through the humility and pain.

Jesus ended his prayer in the garden by telling God the Father that even though he had misgivings about the sacrifice, ultimately, he desired his Father's will, not his. By choosing the pain and humility of the cross, Jesus chose full surrender, dying to self for his Father's greater purpose.

## The Plan: Death on the Cross

On the cross, Jesus experienced fatigue, cramping, scourging, throbbing pain, a crown of thorns forced into his head (John 19:2), massive blood loss, and asphyxia. It's difficult for us to think about Jesus' pain, but Isaiah gave us a clue about why: so *we could be healed*.

"But he [Jesus] was pierced for our rebellion, crushed
for our sins. He [Jesus] was beaten so we could be
whole. He [Jesus] was whipped so we could be healed"
(Isaiah 53:5 NLT).

Perhaps most excruciating is the anguish in his final cry: "And about the ninth hour Jesus cried out with a loud voice, saying, 'Eli, Eli, lema sabachthani?' that is, 'My God, my God, why have you forsaken me?'" (Matthew 27:46).

Jesus felt separation from his Father. God did not liberate Jesus from the cross because his life was the required sacrifice for the redemption of mankind's sins. What suffering God must have felt, sending his Son to his death.

"For our sake he [God the Father] made him [Jesus the
Son] to be sin who knew no sin, so that in him [Jesus]
we might become the righteousness of God"
(2 Corinthians 5:21).

If Jesus had disobeyed his Father, every human being would be condemned to eternal destruction in hell. We would have experienced the horror of what Jesus endured physically, emotionally, and spiritually.

## The Plan: Blood Sacrifice

In the Old Testament, the blood of near-perfect animals was the sacrifice required by God's law to pay for sin. This ritual, performed by the Jewish priests, was a harbinger of the coming Messiah who would save his people. Jesus was the perfect (John 1:29) and final sacrifice to rescue humanity from sin. Paul's letter to the Hebrews explains the significance of God's plan through Jesus:

> "For if the blood of goats and bulls, and the sprinkling
> of defiled persons with the ashes of a heifer, sanctify for
> the purification of the flesh, how much more will the
> blood of Christ, who through the eternal Spirit offered
> himself without blemish to God, purify our conscience
> from dead works to serve the living God?"
> (Hebrews 9:13–14).

The blood of Jesus paid the price for your sins and your freedom. The Old Testament refers to the sacrifice as *atonement*, an action that makes amends for crimes or sin. In modern times, we can temporarily atone for lying by confessing or for stealing by serving jail time. But Jesus' sacrifice on the cross permanently frees those who believe in him as savior. Once your spirit is led by the Holy Spirit, your soul is unburdened by the weight of poor choices.

One of the most influential scriptures in my walk with Jesus comes from Revelation, "And they have conquered him by the blood of the Lamb and by the word of their testimony" (Revelation 12:11). This truth provides you with a powerful weapon to combat mental or emotional attacks from Satan. Our *testimony* is to tell others what Jesus did for all mankind through his sacrifice—Satan was *conquered* by *the blood of the Lamb*.

## The Plan: Resurrected Alive

Grief-stricken followers of Jesus lost hope and assumed his crucifixion ended his message. But God orchestrated the miraculous. He raised

Jesus from the dead and resurrected him to life, fulfilling the promise Jesus shared with his friend Martha prior to his death: "Jesus said to her, 'I am the resurrection and the life. Whoever believes in me, though he die, yet shall he live, and everyone who lives and believes in me shall never die. Do you believe this?'" (John 11:25–26).

For more than forty days following his resurrection, Jesus revealed himself to many people in Jerusalem (Acts 1:3). The nail holes in his feet and hands were visible proof of his sacrifice on the cross (John 20:25).

The foundational truths separating Christianity from other worldviews and religions are the cross and the resurrection. After Jesus died, they buried him in a tomb. But three days later, his Father resurrected him, bringing him back to life. Only Christianity acknowledges and celebrates a resurrected Savior and provides evidence through scriptural references and historical facts (Acts 10:39–41). The religious figureheads and founders of all other faiths are dead and remain in their graves.

Even Satan mistakenly assumed Jesus' death was a victory for evil in the heavenly spiritual war. In a similar way, he wants you to think he is victorious over you by lying about your victory in salvation.

Do you believe Jesus is the resurrection and the life? It took me twenty-seven years to believe this. I believed in God. But I struggled to understand Jesus, his sacrifice for my sin and his resurrection. Through my striving and loss, God patiently revealed his message will never change. It remains God's victory—and therefore, your victory—forever.


## The Plan: Purpose Fulfilled

In his last words spoken from the cross, Jesus revealed the completion of his work of redemption:

"After this, Jesus, knowing that all was now finished,
said (to fulfill the Scripture), 'I thirst.' A jar full of sour
wine stood there, so they put a sponge full of the sour
wine on a hyssop branch and held it to his mouth.
When Jesus had received the sour wine, he said, 'It is
finished,' and he bowed his head and gave up his spirit"
(John 19:28–30).

He came to earth and voluntarily submitted to anguish, abandonment, wrongful accusation, persecution, and death. Why? To save us from the cost of our sins. To show us how to die to self in order to live.

Rising to life after death, Jesus was victorious over sin and death. Forty days later, Jesus returned to heaven, where he sits at the right hand of his Father and prays for you constantly (Romans 8:34).

## The Plan: Return Promised

The book of Acts points to the return of Jesus, which many refer to as his "second coming." To those who witnessed Jesus' ascension to heaven, two angels said:

"Men of Galilee, why do you stand looking into heaven?
This Jesus, who was taken up from you into heaven, will
come in the same way as you saw him go into heaven"
(Acts 1:11).

The book of Revelation outlines unfulfilled prophecies. When Jesus returns, he will establish his heavenly kingdom on earth and bind the work of Satan and his demons forever by casting them into hell. Those who believe in Jesus as Lord and Savior will experience eternal life with God the Father and Jesus the Son. He will forever free his followers from temptation, sins, evil, physical and mental ailments, anguish, and everything meaningless under the sun.

We long for this freedom as we wait expectantly for Jesus to return. But his life must serve as the perfect example of how to walk the narrow path with God now. Our words and actions should reflect our hope that Jesus will return.

## The Plan: Life Abundant

Here's your takeaway, the significance of the cross. Circle this. Write it out.

What happened at the cross is important for you as a follower because what dies at the cross is resurrected to life:

"For the message of the cross is foolishness to those who are perishing, but to us who are being saved it is the power of God" (1 Corinthians 1:18 NIV).

As you continue your walk, Jesus will lead you to surrender your sin and struggles at the cross where the Enemy has no power. Does this surrender mean your sins will be gone forever? Jesus desires sinlessness for you, but your humanness often prompts you to battle your sins and failures in your strength, not his.

Stand firm in the confidence that the cross of Christ sets you free. Surrender those areas to Jesus. Allow him to free you from your sinfulness to experience abundant life.

## Communion: Celebration of the Plan

Communion celebrates all Jesus did through his sacrifice on the cross, giving of himself completely to pay your sin debt so you may have a new life and a restored relationship with God. Communion is not a ritual; rather, it is a symbolic participation in the life, death, and resurrection of Christ, as instructed by Paul through the words of Jesus:

> "For I [apostle Paul] received from the Lord what I also delivered to you, that the Lord Jesus on the night when he was betrayed took bread, and when he had given thanks, he broke it, and said, 'This is my body, which is for you. Do this in remembrance of me.' In the same way also he took the cup, after supper, saying, 'This cup is the new covenant in my blood. Do this, as often as you drink it, in remembrance of me.' For as often as you eat this bread and drink the cup, you proclaim the Lord's death until he comes" (1 Corinthians 11:23–26).

The *bread* of the communion celebration represents the body of Jesus, broken once on the cross. The *cup,* filled with wine or juice, represents the blood of Jesus, poured out at the cross for the atonement of your sins.

Paul told the people of Corinth, the celebration of communion is solely intended for followers of Jesus.

> "Whoever, therefore, eats the bread or drinks the cup of the Lord in an unworthy manner will be guilty concerning the body and blood of the Lord. Let a person examine himself, then, and so eat of the bread and drink of the cup" (1 Corinthians 11:27–28).

Jesus encourages you to participate in communion consistently— alone or with others, in both difficult and joyous times. You don't have to be in a church building to take part in communion. Jesus is less concerned about the actual method of serving and receiving communion than he is about its relevance and meaning in your life: coming with a clean, humble heart to remember and celebrate him.

The cross means so much more to me than a symbol of Christianity as a religion. When Jesus hung on the cross, God's holiness clashed with Satan's evil and hatred for humanity. The cross reveals how radical God can be to save us from the penalty of sin. Through the cross, God crushed Satan's power and restored those who believe in Jesus to a right relationship with him. The cross represents the fulfillment of the purpose of Jesus' life: to die so we may live. The cross changed everything about the human condition two thousand years ago, and its power continues to change us today.

## Take Action

**1.** Think of a time you made a sacrifice, or someone made one for you. Journal the reasons for the sacrifice and the outcomes? How does this sacrifice change your understanding of the cross?

**2.** Make a list of possessions, attitudes, people, or mindsets you think Jesus may ask you to surrender at the cross?

## Next Step on the Path

How are you connected to Jesus? Read John 7:38 to gain insight for the next chapter.

## Chapter Six

# How Can I Feel Connected to God?

God invites us to intimately connect with his heart and Spirit.

December 15, 2003, is a day I will never forget. After years of pain, my mom lost her battle with Parkinson's disease. Her seventy-pound frail body lay in a hospice bed at my sister's home. Although I thought I was ready emotionally for Mom to die, nothing prepared me for what happened when she passed.

My sister woke me that morning with the news Mom was gone. When I entered her room, I realized though her body lay in the bed, something was missing—her life. The unique part of Mom that was special to me was gone.

Hours after the coroner left, my sister and I talked about Mom. I shared an experience that had occurred days prior to Mom's passing.

As I sat quietly beside her, I looked over just in time to witness a peaceful smile at the corners of her mouth. In those moments, the anxiety Mom had battled for years seemed to subside.

I leaned close to her ear and whispered, "Mom?"

"Yes, Scott," she replied in a barely audible voice.

"Do you see Jesus?"

With a long, breathy whisper, she responded, "Yesssss."

Jesus was revealing himself to my mom. Overwhelmed by the joy and sorrow I felt simultaneously, I wept as I prayed for her, asking Jesus to take her home.

Now that he had, I wasn't sure what to feel.

Later the night of Mom's passing, I curled up on my sister's sofa in a fetal position. I sobbed, almost unable to breathe because the emotional agony became physical. The pain became a forceful undercurrent deep inside me, sucking the life out of my chest and right through my back, leaving a vast emptiness in its wake. I called out to Jesus, "Please, help me!" Finally, I cried myself to sleep.

When the piercing sunlight through the window woke me the following morning, I gathered my belongings and headed out to my car for the three-hour drive home. On the way, I vacillated between talking, screaming, and crying out to Jesus. Then a radical change took place within me.

Something great and powerful, something supernatural—far beyond anything I had ever experienced—filled the cavern of emptiness my mother's death had opened inside me. Jesus poured an emotional healing into me that felt like a physical filling of cool water. The peaceful presence of Jesus engulfed me, cleansed me, restored me. I had a fuller, fresher understanding of what Jesus meant when he said, "Whoever believes in me [Jesus], as the Scripture has said, 'Out of his heart will flow rivers of living water'" (John 7:38).

Years later, Jesus revealed the mystery of what I experienced with Mom's passing: a glimpse into the deep bond between the human spiritual heart with God's heart and Spirit. Through this revelation, I understood more fully the connection of the human spiritual heart can be traced back to the relationship Adam and Eve had with God as they walked with him in the garden of Eden, prior to the fall.

## From Life to Death

Adam and Eve walked naked, unashamed, and free in relationship with God. They had nothing to hide because they were pure and holy. To be holy simply means to be set apart for God's calling and purpose. Adam and Eve had true communion with God. Their hearts were right with him and his love and presence filled them.

God invited Adam and Eve to enjoy the garden and everything in it, except for one tree:

> "And the LORD God commanded the man, saying, 'You may surely eat of every tree of the garden, but of the tree of the knowledge of good and evil you shall not eat, for in the day that you eat of it you shall surely die'" (Genesis 2:16–17).

Despite what they knew, Adam and Eve ate from the forbidden tree when Satan, in the form of a serpent, offered them an alternative. They chose sin over obedience, pride over humility, and self over God.

Repetitive sin results in sin patterns (as discussed in the Introduction). Adam and Eve went from walking in abundant life with God to separation, fear and distance from God.

When the wide path that leads to destruction unfolded before them, Adam and Eve detoured from their walk with God and died instantly. But their death was not physical; they died spiritually. What does spiritual death mean? Their relationship and communion with God was severed.

Immediately following their disobedience, Adam and Eve felt both shame and guilt, so they tried to cover up the mess they created.

Are they any different from you or me?

They lost their life compass, yielded to fear, and played the blame game. Even though their spirits were dead to God, they were still physically alive and exposed to the evil of the world.

The Bible tells us when Adam and Eve sinned, every human being, including you and me, lost the vital life connection, or *spirit connection*, to our heavenly Father—God. Therefore, every person is born into this disconnected, or fallen, state.

## From Death to Life

Believing God exists will not bridge the separation. Your spirit remains disconnected from God and lies dormant within you until you give your heart to Jesus. By believing in him through faith, your spirit is quickened (instantaneously responsive) and reconnected to your life source in God. In your fallen, dormant state, you survive through your fallen spirit, using your mind, will, and emotions (your soul) and your body (physical being) as you interact with the world.

In this state you cannot flourish, because your spirit is separated from God. Do not buy into the world's definition of *flourish*, meaning prosperous or wealthy. Instead, think of flourishing as living with an eternal purpose for God, as your spirit communes with him.

## Defining Spirit, Soul, and Body

Let's explore my experience with Mom's passing to explain the spiritual heart. The loss I described, that sucking feeling, occurred within my spiritual heart. Your spiritual heart consists of your spirit, soul, and body, which should work together to draw you close to God and enable you to love others. Each person's DNA is different; likewise, each person's spiritual heart is different.

The pain of Mom's death stayed with me a long time. My emotions wavered from tearing up or laughing inexplicably at a memory. Peppered in with regrets of the things I never said. In those moments, God drew me near to him. Months passed before I could focus on the peace and healing God provided. And the hope of seeing Mom again in heaven. Because God created our spiritual hearts differently, my emotional healing was a shorter journey than it may be for someone else.

From what we've discussed about Adam and Eve and my experience with Mom's passing, we can better understand how God created you:

**The spiritual heart** defines who you are. It is your personality—the unique part of you that makes you different from everyone else.

**The spirit** is your life's connection to God that comes alive within you when you believe in Jesus as Lord. This is your spiritual life with Jesus.

**The soul** consists of mind, will, and emotions. You process thoughts in your mind, your will determines how you respond to those thoughts, and your emotions influence how you react behaviorally to those thoughts.

**The body** is your physical being through which you engage and respond to the five senses—tasting, hearing, touching, seeing, and smelling. Your reaction to these senses affects your will and emotions and influences your decisions, including your sinful urges, also referred to as the flesh.

## Connected to God through the Spirit

God loves you and desires a relationship with you. Because communication is vital in any relationship, the Holy Spirit communicates with you through your spirit, providing guidance, warnings, and insight.

Man's spiritual bond with God is similar to the life a mother provides her child in the womb through the umbilical cord. As long as the umbilical cord is healthy and connected, the child receives life-sustaining nutrients. Without this vital attachment the child would die. This physical link also provides warmth and safety, and demonstrates the mother's love for the child. Without the spirit connection—our spiritual umbilical cord—human beings cannot experience eternal life with God; neither can we know the love of our heavenly Father and Creator.

Since you are spiritually connected with God, why is it you don't *want* to sin, but you still battle the *urge* to sin?

The apostle Paul dealt with this question of sinful urges in his life. In Romans 7:15 (ESV) he wrote, "I do not understand my own actions. For I do not do what I want, but I do the very thing I hate." He adds in verse 17, "So now it is no longer I who do it, but sin that dwells within me."

Because of the spiritual detachment, or death, that entered the world when Adam and Eve sinned, human beings pursue everything under the sun to feel alive again, just as Solomon and Paul both observed. The wide path Solomon followed led to destruction. But eventually he realized, out of all his possessions, the most important treasure was his spirit's relationship with God (Ecclesiastes 12:7). In Romans 8:2, Paul shares what he had learned about the Holy Spirit's power over sin: "For the law of the Spirit of life has set you free in Christ

Jesus from the law of sin and death." Only the power of the Holy Spirit can overcome the sin in our life.

## Connected to God through a Relationship with Jesus

The next relationship we will explore is your connection to God through Jesus. Your spirit is quickened [brought to life] with God, "if you confess with your mouth that Jesus is Lord and believe in your heart that God raised him from the dead, you will be saved" (Romans 10:9). This bond with Jesus is a prerequisite to living with an eternal vision, directed by God himself. This amazing journey is difficult, though, and *those who find it are few*, as the Bible warns in Matthew 7:14.

Now that we've established the importance of this connection with Jesus, is Jesus calling you into an intentional, intimate relationship with him? Ask him to make all things new in your heart by filling the voids with his love. Let go of the past and speak these words to Jesus:

Jesus, please forgive me for living my life for myself,
even after I know you have cleansed me of my sins.
Please remove my guilt and shame and take me back
into your loving arms. I recommit my heart and mind
to walk with you. Father, lead me, challenge me, and
grow me as I choose to walk with you. I want to learn
why I struggle the way I do and how to overcome these
struggles through your guidance. In your name, I pray.
Amen (which means to agree).

Jesus heard you and will respond. Do not anticipate what the response will look like. Simply believe that he will answer. Allow him to heal, correct, lead, and restore your heart. Your part is to focus on Jesus. Take one step at a time, nurturing your vital relationship with Jesus and experience a new beginning in him.

## Heart Transformation through a Relationship with Jesus

Some may think, as I first did, believing in Jesus makes your heart right with him immediately. Not true. Your spirit connection to God restores instantly when you confess your sins and accept Jesus as savior. Your spiritual heart undergoes a transformation process, however, as God aligns your heart with his and changes every part of your being. Your will calibrates with his will. The Bible refers to this transformation as sanctification:

"Now may the God of peace himself sanctify you completely, and may your whole spirit and soul and body be kept blameless at the coming of our Lord Jesus Christ. He who calls you is faithful; he will surely do it" (1 Thessalonians 5:23–24).

In chapter 3, I define *sanctification* as set apart or free from sin. The Holy Spirit works to separate you from sin and the habits, ways, and thoughts keeping you on the destructive path. Sanctification is an ongoing process to keep your heart right with God and free from sin's bondage.

The experience of losing my mom was one of the most vulnerable points of my life, but never once did God allow me to feel awkward or alone. Our great and powerful Creator was so deeply personal in my darkest moments—he comforted me and allowed the Spirit to provide healing in my spiritual heart. This intimate time with him forged a deep bond between his Spirit and my spirit, his heart to my heart, Father to child. Your relationship with Jesus can connect you to God in this way, too, once you invite the Spirit into the recesses of your spiritual heart.

## Take Action

**1.** Describe what you felt when you first gave your heart to Jesus.

**2.** What makes your relationship with Jesus more extraordinary than anything else you've experienced?

## Next Step on the Path

Why is it important to study the Bible? Read 2 Timothy 3:16–17 to prepare for the next chapter.

*Chapter Seven*

# How Does the Bible Help Me?

**The Bible grounds our faith and provides instruction for life.**

After I purchased an emergency home generator, I read the lengthy owner's manual. But one section made me double back: the book stressed the need to ground the generator in case of a power surge strong enough to back up into the system. Failure to ground the generator properly could cause mechanical damage and personal injury—even death.

Grounding protects the generator from unanticipated electrical current through a wire and metal rod hammered into the ground. The need for grounding concerned me at first. I wondered if the potential danger associated with a generator was the right choice for my family. After I spoke with experts and understood the *how* and *why* of safe generator usage, my fear subsided.

As valuable as the generator would be in an emergency, it would be useless if I left it in the box. And if I neglected to read the manual and follow the instructions, not only would I miss the maximum potential of powering our home, but I also could have caused immense harm to the machine and to myself.

My experience with the generator reminds me of the Bible. At first, investing time in Bible reading was cumbersome. What part should I read first? How can a book written thousands of years ago apply to my life today? I learned how reading and applying only portions of the Bible could be dangerous, but if I allow the Bible to speak into my life and ground me, it will be a "lamp to my feet and a light to my path" (Psalm 119:105).

## Your Worldview Matters

What and who you listen to are important. Your beliefs chart the course of your journey, whether you're walking the wide path that leads to destruction or the narrow path that leads to life. What you consider truth establishes your worldview—a network of beliefs and suppositions forming your life philosophy and the legacy you leave for others.

We live in a culture far removed from biblical truth. Clergy water down God's Word in exchange for preaching prosperity. Politicians appease voters rather than embody justice for the good of our nation. Journalists suppress the truth and subject us to their personal agenda.

The salvation message of Jesus Christ grounds *Why Can't I Get This Jesus Thing Right?* in biblical truth, the cornerstone of our faith. God's Word will never change. It is not based on trends or fads, cultural influences, or even world leadership. Jesus prayed, "Sanctify them in the truth; your word is truth" (John 17:17). Truth, therefore, is a fixed standard, an absolute. Gravity, mathematics, the annual calendar, the earth's axis to the sun, and seasonal changes are examples of fixed standards. Biblical truth is constant and eternal; therefore, the Bible provides the authoritative guidelines Christians live by. We cannot alter this truth without consequence (Revelation 22:18).

The Bible is the genuine, living, and spoken Word of God: "Above all, you must understand that no prophecy of Scripture came about by the prophet's own interpretation of things. For prophecy never had its origin in the human will, but prophets, though human, spoke from God as they were carried along by the Holy Spirit" (2 Peter 1:20–21 NIV). The Bible is as effective and relevant today as it was in biblical times: "For the word of God is living and active, sharper than any two-edged sword, piercing to the division of soul and of spirit, of joints and of marrow, and discerning the thoughts and intentions of the heart" (Hebrews 4:12).

## God's Word: The Promises

The Pentateuch is the first five books of the Bible, authored by Moses. It was assembled between 1450 BC and 1410 BC—3,500 years ago—and ends with the fifth book of the Bible, Deuteronomy. It summarizes God's laws and promises: if God's people bless him, he will pour out his goodness and benevolence on them, beyond human comprehension (Deuteronomy 11:26–28). To bless God means to love him, repent of your sins, and seek him with all your heart, then follow him and faithfully walk in his truth (John 14:21).

God promised his people when they blessed him, he would restore their nation, and they would be safe from their enemies. Their work would prosper, families would thrive, and their destiny would be held safely in his hands. God reaffirmed that promise to Joshua when he succeeded Moses as leader of the nation:

> "This Book of the Law shall not depart from your mouth, but you shall meditate on it day and night, so that you may be careful to do according to all that is written in it. For then you will make your way prosperous, and then you will have good success" (Joshua 1:8).

The opposite was also true. If the people cursed God—turned from his ways, renounced his truth, and sought *after other gods*—God swore curses would fall on them. These curses meant God would remove his favor and his protection from their enemies.

## God's Word: The Foundation

All sturdy walls need a strong foundation. At the base of each foundation is a cornerstone that joins the initial two walls of the structure. Thousands of years ago, Paul used this analogy to help us understand God's Word as the foundation of our faith:

> "So then you are no longer strangers and aliens [non-believers], but you are fellow citizens with the saints and members of the household of God [Church], built on the foundation of the apostles and prophets, Christ Jesus himself being the cornerstone, in whom the whole structure, being joined together, grows into a holy temple in the Lord. In him you also are being built together into a dwelling place for God by the Spirit"
> (Ephesians 2:19–22).

Everything you study in God's Word points to Jesus as the *cornerstone* of your faith. Rather than secluding you from the world, your walls of faith prepare and protect a holy place within your heart. The Word of God is living and active, constantly revealing God's mysteries through the life, love, and hope found only in Jesus Christ. "In the beginning was the Word [Jesus], and the Word was with God, and the Word was God. He was in the beginning with God. All things were made through him, and without him was not any thing made that was made. In him was life, and the life was the light of men. The light shines in the darkness, and the darkness has not overcome it" (John 1:1–5).

God's Word illustrates the kingdom of heaven through numerous pictures of the wonders and magnificent glory of God and what is yet to come—our eternal home with the Father, Son, and Holy Spirit for all followers. Today, you are fortunate to have the Bible assembled in its complete, final form of sixty-six books so you can chart your course daily on your journey with Jesus. God's Word is always fresh, and through it Jesus transforms us, providing revelatory clarity, direction, and wisdom.

God's Word can measure the correctness and validity of everything we hear and see. It contains God's precepts (commands to act on), and his boundaries (guidelines for your steps of faith), so you do not stumble over the rocky terrain of life's circumstances. Your hunger for God's Word should mirror the psalmist's. "Lead me in your truth and teach me, for you are the God of my salvation; for you I wait all the day long" (Psalm 25:5).

## God's Word: The Purpose

I needed to read the generator manual to understand its purpose and uses; similarly, you need to read the Bible to understand your purpose and usefulness:

> "All Scripture is breathed out by God and profitable for teaching, for reproof, for correction, and for training in righteousness, that the man of God may be complete, equipped for every good work" (2 Timothy 3:16–17).

The passage above outlines God's purpose for the Bible and how it should be engaged. The Bible is beneficial for:

➤ *Teaching:* to provide tools and principles so you can learn how to walk the narrow path with Jesus.

➤ *Reproof:* to reprimand, or admonish, in love; to help you consider choices and actions that might lead you onto the wide path of destruction.

➤ *Correction:* to make right a wrong action or belief.

➤ *Training:* to prepare you to walk faithfully, according to God's Word, and to live with an eternal vision.

That is the *why* and *what* of the Bible. What about the *how* and its practical usage?

**God's Word: The Application**

To simplify your journey through the Bible, here are three approaches:

**Teaching Settings:** In addition to attending church, take classes taught by trained teachers who impart the true Word of God and create an environment for students to learn from both the teacher and one another. Paul gave young Pastor Timothy the following counsel, "Until I come, devote yourself to the public reading of Scripture, to exhortation [being urged to act upon something that you hear], to teaching" (1 Timothy 4:13).

**Group Settings:** Matthew 18:20 says when "two or three are gathered" to focus on Jesus, he is present. Group settings are more intimate than a congregation or classroom and allow the participants to ask questions and give more personal responses. "Do your best to present yourself to God as one approved, a worker who has no need to be ashamed, rightly handling the word of truth" (2 Timothy 2:15). "One approved" refers to a person who has walked through life's challenges with Jesus and remained faithful. In this setting, the group members typically know and have learned to trust one another. Deeper revelation of God's Word may evolve in these settings, as it encourages personal interaction while participants gird one another in God's truth.

**Individual Study:** Studying God's Word with others is profitable, but the most fertile soil for your growth comes through the personal time you spend with God in the Word. Joshua 1:8 tells you to "meditate on it day and night, so that you may be careful to do according to all that is written in it." To meditate is to think deeply, to focus your mind on bite-size portions of the Bible. In these times, open your heart to God so he can speak revelations about what you read. Use the psalmist's prayer to prepare your heart. "Open my eyes, that I may behold wondrous things out of your law" (Psalm 119:18).

When you approach God's Word as his love letter, written over thousands of years, it becomes his journal, expressing the unfathomable depths of his heart. Jesus said, "If you abide in my word, you are truly my disciples, and you will know the truth, and the truth will set you free" (John 8:31–32). To experience this freedom, immerse yourself in God's Word. Follow Paul's advice to Timothy "Think over what I say, for the Lord will give you understanding in everything" (2 Timothy 2:7).

What could Paul's advice to *think over what I say* look like for you?

## Reading and Studying God's Word

First, understand the difference between reading and studying. Reading the Bible daily immerses your spirit in God's Word and builds familiarity with its truth. Studying the Bible encourages spiritual growth and deeper insight. Let's consider these approaches separately: Daily Reading and Studying.

## Daily Reading

Nourishing your soul daily in the Bible is like giving your physical body food. The books of the Bible are not arranged in chronological order, so you don't need to begin with the Old Testament and read chapter by chapter.

Start with a shorter book of the New Testament. As your Bible's Table of Contents shows, the New Testament begins with the four gospels—Matthew, Mark, Luke, and John—followed by the book of Acts. After Acts come the Pauline epistles, or letters written by the apostle Paul. These letters include Romans, 1 and 2 Corinthians, Galatians, Ephesians, Philippians, Colossians, 1 and 2 Thessalonians, 1 and 2 Timothy, Titus, and Philemon. Once you read through a short book, such as Philemon, choose another book similar in length, so you become familiar with the scriptural language.

A one-year reading plan is simple to follow and establishes a goal to complete your readings. Many online Bible reading plans are available. Some courses suggest a daily reading of small sections of the Old Testament (history and prophecy), Psalms (poetry), Proverbs (wisdom), coupled with the New Testament (the life and teachings of Jesus and events of the early New Testament Church).

The goal is not to read through the Bible to accomplish a task. Instead, allow the Holy Spirit to speak into your soul about the *living and active* truth of the Bible.

## Studying

Examining and meditating on God's Word requires time, discipline, and an action plan. The intent of biblical study is to dig deep into the Word and allow Scripture to interpret Scripture. In this way, you allow God's Word to reveal its profound, never-changing truth rather than allowing your opinions to mislead you.

While serving as a missionary in the Ukraine, I completed a nine-month inductive Bible study course taught through the School of Biblical Studies (SBS)/Youth With A Mission (YWAM). This course profoundly impacted my method of studying the Bible, especially I applied historical background to understand relevant truth today. *How to Read the Bible for All Its Worth* by Gordon D. Fee and Douglas

Stuart is a good resource, which will give you tools to understand how to study the Bible.

Just as the generator manual provided exactly what I needed to understand its purpose and uses, the Bible is our manual for life. Through the Bible, Jesus has opened my eyes and grounded my faith. Like the psalmist says,

> "The law [Bible] of the LORD is perfect, reviving the soul; the testimony of the LORD is sure, making wise the simple; the precepts of the LORD are right, rejoicing the heart; the commandment of the LORD is pure, enlightening the eyes" (Psalm 19:7–8).

The Bible is *perfect, sure, wise, right* and *pure.* Approaching God's Word with this mind-set revives your soul and provides opportunity for God's discernment.

## Action Step

1. What was one point that helped you recognize the relevance of the Bible in a different way?

**2.** What's one step you can take to engage deeper in studying God's Word?

## Next Step on the Path

What do you know about your Enemy, Satan? Read Isaiah 14:12–15 in the English Standard Version to prepare for the next chapter.

# PART TWO

# Understanding Your Enemy

"The thief [Satan] comes only to steal and kill
and destroy" (John 10:10a).

## Chapter Eight

# Why Do I Need to Know About Satan?

**The Bible tells us Satan is the father of all lies.**

The clear blue waters and mild weather of Costa Rica created the perfect setting for sitting atop a fishing rig. My family and I began the day with one goal in mind: to catch a salt-water marlin that would possibly elicit the fight of our life. The anticipation of reeling in this large fish, using all our strength to draw him to the boat, followed by the liberating euphoria of setting him free, generated intense excitement as we prepared ourselves for the day.

We set sail toward a fishing spot the captain insisted would improve our chances of a catch. Once the boat reached trawling speed—a little faster than a jogging pace—the captain instructed us to release our lines into the water. The boat's speed drew the line from the reel taut, as the weight of the bait and hook submerged a few feet below the sea's surface.

Boom! Our line was hit. Our heads jerked up. The tight line signaled we had hooked a marlin. We felt its strength on the other end—pulling desperately away from us. The reel spun, almost uncontrollably, as the marlin yanked the line. When the magnificent five-foot creature surfaced, we gasped. We battled the seventy-pound fish with a fishing rod that seemed ridiculously inadequate.

We reeled in our catch, making sure the line did not grow too tight or too loose. About twenty-five minutes later, we brought the large fish alongside the boat. We relished the thrill of the catch and marveled how one small hook landed that enormous fish. Its fate rested in our hands … simply because it took the bait.

## Satan, the Great Adversary

Just as the marlin took the bait in my family's fishing experience, Satan, your enemy, baits multiple hooks to tempt you. The adversary of both God and man, Satan will do whatever he can to capture you with a baited hook. Then he will destroy you.

Although the Bible records much information about Satan, his demons, and their work, few churches and Christian groups discuss his person and methods. Jesus warned us of Satan and his intentions in John 10:10, "the thief comes only to steal and kill and destroy."

The Bible also refers to him as Lucifer, Day Star or Morning Star, and Devil. Satan was once a powerful member of the angelic host within God's kingdom. Discontented with God's blessings, gifts, and his position in God's kingdom, Satan's pride and greed drove him to desire God's authority. Because of his rebellion, God cast Satan and "a third of the stars [angels] of heaven" out of his presence (Revelation 12:3–14). Although it is unclear what a third of the angels represents numerically, we can assume a great multitude followed Satan. God banished these fallen angels, or demons, from his kingdom forever.

Isaiah 14:12–15 recounts the fall of Satan. The text refers to the upheaval of a dictator who was a king of Babylon. Biblical scholars also believe this text describes Satan's fall from heaven. Satan's prideful attempt to gain authority over God brought him down to *Sheol*, also called the pit of darkness or hell. "You said in your heart, I will ascend to heaven; above the stars of God I will set my throne on high" (Isaiah 14:13a).

The declaration "I will," stated five times in the Isaiah passage, reveals Satan's pride, which caused his fall from heaven. This sin guarantees his absolute destruction, and it was the first broad stroke of the scythe that blazed the wide path to destruction (Matthew 7:13). His proud heart and haughty spirit cost him everything. He allowed greed for God's power to overcome him. War then erupted in the heavens and has continued throughout time because "pride goes before destruction, and a haughty spirit before a fall" (Proverbs 16:18).

## What Are Some of Satan's Characteristics?

Satan hates God; therefore, he hates every follower. Hate is a strong word, but it is precisely what drives the Enemy to seek control of your heart. God is omniscient, knows everything, and omnipresent, everywhere at the same time. But Satan is not! He does, however, exercise tremendous power and accomplishes his work through demons (Matthew 12:24; Revelation 12:7–9).

Below is an abbreviated list of Satan's characteristics, describing his capabilities and how he may work in your life. Focusing on these characteristics too long can overwhelm you. Learn from this list but keep your eyes on Jesus.

## Satan is THE...

> ➤ *Enemy* (Matthew 13:25, 28, 39) who thrives on destruction by wreaking havoc in your life.

- *Murderer* (John 8:44) who pursues your death mentally, emotionally, and physically.

- *Deceiver* (Revelation 20:10) who tries to confuse you about what is right and wrong.

- *Tempter* (1 Thessalonians 3:5) who appeals to your weakness to draw you into sin and toward him.

- *Wicked one, evil one* (Matthew 6:13; Matthew 13:19, 38; 1 John 2:13) who fights against the truth, opposes Jesus, and causes chaos in this world through his malicious acts of wickedness.

- *False accuser of those who follow Jesus Christ* (Revelation 12:10) who convinces you to walk in self-condemnation, continual shame, and guilt because of your past sins, mistakes, and failures.

- *Ruler of this world* (John 12:31); *god of this age* (2 Corinthians 4:4); *prince of the power of the air* (Ephesians 2:2)—each title reveals his control over the world and its current state.

## How Does Satan Use Temptation to Bait You?

Temptation is a strategically baited hook the Enemy sets before you to lure or feed the unsanctified parts of your heart. These heart voids entice you to fill your selfish needs and desires rather than remain faithful and obedient to God. Typically, temptation is an action or thought that has previously led you into sin, such as the ones Paul lists in the book of Galatians:

> "Now the works of the flesh are evident: sexual immorality, impurity, sensuality, idolatry, sorcery, enmity, strife, jealousy, fits of anger, rivalries, dissensions, divisions, envy, drunkenness,

orgies, and things like these. I warn you, as I warned
you before, that those who do such things will
not inherit the kingdom of God"
(Galatians 5:19–21).

Some say sin is in the eye of the beholder. Others consider themselves to be free from sin. But human beings do not define sin, neither do societal influences or religious organizations. The Bible and God's commandments determine what is and is not sin. And no person is sinless, even those who profess Jesus as Lord and Savior:

"If we say we have no sin, we deceive ourselves, and the
truth is not in us. If we confess our sins, he is faithful
and just to forgive us our sins and to cleanse us from all
unrighteousness. If we say we have not sinned, we make
him [Jesus] a liar, and his word is not in us"
(1 John 1:8–10).

Even though you may long to be free from sin, you will still sin. Years ago, I battled the sin of lust—lust for more in my career, marriage, and possessions. I asked God why my thoughts kept drawing me back to that sin. God stunned me with this thought, "Because you love yourself more than you love me." Each time I gravitated back to my sin, I chose myself over God. I did not want to push God aside, but my body warred against my soul. Paul describes a similar struggle:

"For I do not understand my own actions. For I do
not do what I want, but I do the very thing I hate.... 
So now it is no longer I who do it, but sin that dwells
within me. For I know that nothing good dwells in me,

that is, in my flesh. For I have the desire to do what is
right, but not the ability to carry it out. For I do not
do the good I want, but the evil I do not want is what
I keep on doing. Now if I do what I do not want, it is
no longer I who do it, but sin that dwells within me"
(Romans 7:15, 17–20).

What's the difference between temptation and sin? Temptation is an
attempt to lead you to sin. Rather than focusing on the bait, be aware
of your weak areas so you can be on guard against Satan's schemes.
Once you have fallen to temptation and the hook of sin has captured
you, like the marlin, you cannot free yourself. Only Jesus can set
you free. Only he can deliver you from the spiritual bondage that
ensnares you.

During our Costa Rican fishing expedition, my family and I freed
the marlin from the hook. Satan, however, will not let you off the
hook—whether you commit a single act of sin or experience a life-
changing failure. I have walked the path of destruction and know
how devastating separation from God feels. Even after I chose to
follow Jesus, I followed the wide path. That's why all of us must equip
ourselves to understand the Enemy and his tactics.

## How Can Satan Influence You?

The Enemy does not work alone. He has a powerful army. We will
expand on this topic in chapter 9 but these evil forces will not stop
their attacks. They will continue hurling thoughts and temptations
until you stop responding to them in unhealthy, habitual ways. But
there is good news: Satan and his cronies can only shoot thoughts
into your mind. God alone can read your thoughts and know what
is in your heart.

Satan's *flaming darts,* or thoughts of sinful behavior, are an all-out mental assault. His strategy begins with firing a single arrow into your mind—thoughts of lying, stealing, overeating, inflicting physical harm to yourself or others, illicit sexual behavior, drunkenness, greed, or gossip. He waits to see what you do. If you continue gravitating toward the behavior, more flaming darts will follow. The pattern starts slowly, but the frequency increases, based on your reaction to the thoughts and temptations he sets before you.

If you do not recognize Satan's attack, you will eventually succumb to the temptation. Caught in a downward spiral, you relinquish your faithfulness to Jesus. Your thoughts begin justifying behaviors and their consequences. You may experience a sense of entitlement, as you make a deliberate choice to focus on immediate gratification, while pushing Jesus away: "I deserve this … I need this … I am worthy of this reward … no one will ever know."

At this point you have allowed the thoughts to become a part of your soul, instead of giving them to the One who can set you free—Jesus. Jesus spoke about the power of our thought life and its ability to lead us into sin:

> "But I say to you that everyone who looks at a woman
> [or man] with lustful intent has already committed
> adultery with her [or him] in his heart" (Matthew 5:28).

The worst choice is to follow through with the temptation and engage in the actual sin. While you may reason it away in your mind, remember sin, no matter how large or small it may seem, is still sin. All sin hinders your relationship with Jesus.

How do you thwart the Enemy's attacks? By seizing the flaming arrow before it embeds in your mind. Picture yourself raising your hand above your head, fingers spread wide, capturing the thought in air, as if it were a baseball. Then, release the thought to Jesus, asking him to extinguish its power. At first, this practice takes conscious effort, like training in a new skill. Eventually, you learn to catch the thoughts as a reflex to Satan's attack.

The only way to break the sin patterns in your life is to turn to Jesus and engage his power to deliver you from evil. Jesus gives you a weapon to stand firm in your faith, "In all circumstances take up the shield of faith, with which you can extinguish all the flaming darts of the evil one" (Ephesians 6:16). We will discuss the shield and additional armor with which God equips you in chapter 11.

Although the battle on your soul can be fierce, God limits the Enemy's power. Jesus' power, however, is unlimited and eternal.

## If Satan Has Restrictions, Why Is There So Much Suffering?

Satan goes to great lengths to suppress and distort the message of Jesus and salvation in this world (Matthew 13:19; 1 Thessalonians 2:17–18). He wants to destroy the church and the work of the people who spread the truth of Jesus, the gospel message. *Gospel* means "good news." It proclaims the good news of the forgiveness of sin through the atoning death of Jesus Christ.

Satan has the power to tempt and lead people to sin. You and I can attest to the fact he causes horrendous pain and suffering in the world. But he does not have freedom to destroy anyone he desires. In the story of Job, Satan asked God for permission to afflict this righteous man (Job 1:7–12). Although Job experienced heartbreaking loss and suffering, God was victorious over Satan. Job glorified God through his righteous choices.

Why is there so much pain in this world since God is in control and he does not permit Satan to rule over people and conquer their lives (John 14:30–31)? That question has perplexed followers for centuries. Here's what I know: we live in a sinful world, over which Satan rules. As long as sin and Satan are free to roam this earth, people will suffer.

Sin results from poor choices. Freely roaming thoughts and sin cause destruction and lead to pain and suffering. Even though you follow Jesus, you will experience trials on this side of heaven. Your salvation in Jesus does not insulate you from pain and evil, but it provides the grace and mercy to walk through them.

## How Do You Stand Firm and Remain Unafraid?

The Bible says God is the "Alpha and the Omega—the beginning and the end" (Revelation 22:13). He is victorious both now and for all eternity. Even though the Enemy is powerful, God will eventually imprison him in hell. He will not taunt those who follow Jesus any longer. Even though spiritual battles continue in the heavenly realms, know God is in control. He and his angels will never fall victim to Satan and his demons.

Do not fear the Enemy. Learn to respect his power and recognize how he lures you toward sin. He is battling for your heart. Stay cognizant—not fearful—to protect yourself from his schemes. The Apostle Peter put it this way: "Be sober-minded; be watchful. Your adversary the devil prowls around like a roaring lion, seeking someone to devour" (1 Peter 5:8). Satan wants to completely destroy or ruin your life.

But Satan cannot destroy a believer, which we learned from Job (Job 1:10-12, 42:12-17). His greatest desire is to lure you to sin and keep you from walking closely with Jesus.

Without your spiritual eyes and ears constantly focused on Jesus, you are likely to return to sinful ways. Not only have I witnessed this in those who do not follow Jesus, but I have also seen this in people who have given their lives to Jesus.

Satan tests believers to determine if we are on alert, tempting us with familiar sins, overeating, binge shopping, addictions to alcohol, drugs or porn. This emphasizes the importance of keeping our faith deeply rooted in Jesus.

Although the massive marlin struggled to be free as we reeled it closer to the boat, it became exhausted and succumbed to our control. This once powerful fish was helpless by attractive bait and a simple hook. The longer Satan can keep you on the hook, the more exhausted and hopeless your heart feels. Like the marlin, you will eventually give up on what Jesus desires to do in and through you. You will miss the joy and purpose Jesus created for you.

When we stand firm in our commitment to Jesus and remain wary of Satan's lures, we will not take his bait. Satan is clever and strong, but God is all wise and all powerful. Choose to stay close to God.

## Action Steps

**1.** What bait does Satan use in his attempts to hook you?

**2.** Of the seven characteristics describing Satan, which does he most often use against you? Write out what you believe the long-term effects of his strategy might be.

## Next Step on the Path

As you will learn in the next chapter, your human nature causes you to gravitate toward feeding your sinful nature. Read 1 John 2:16–17 to prepare for the next chapter.

*Chapter Nine*

# Where Am I Vulnerable to Satan?

Temptations are weaknesses leading us to sin.

I spent time in Thailand, a beautiful country rich in tropical beaches, mountain vistas, history, food, and culture. One memorable experience was an elephant ride. As I mounted this powerful creature—weighing close to 12,000 pounds—I was intrigued (and perhaps a little intimidated) to note only a thin rope held this adult elephant in place, which tethered his back leg to a tree. Even though I knew the elephants were well trained and would not wander away, I also understood the elephant could snap the rope like a piece of thread if he so desired. Why didn't he?

Nearby stood an elephant calf. He was less than a year old, about one-third the size of the adult male and chained to a solid wood post. The calf pulled at the chain, attempting to free itself. I asked the trainer about the young elephant. He explained how they chain the calves to the post to condition them into believing they cannot break loose. He also said, "The calves eventually give up and stop pulling on the chain. They are then submissive to their circumstances for the rest of their lives."

The same principle applies to sin and your vulnerability to Satan. You may believe your cannot break the spiritual chains, so you succumb to sin, habits, and defeat. Satan conditions you to believe he will dominate the rest of your life, like the elephant chained to the post.

Let's look at various ways the Enemy can make you feel as if you are chained to him.

## How Does Satan Hold You in Bondage?

Sin is an unintentional or deliberate act of disobedience against God, which results in separation or independence from God. Sin falls into two broad categories—sins of omission and sins of commission:

> ➤ Sins of omission are unintentional acts. They are neither premeditated nor deliberate. Here are some examples: flying into a fit of rage or jealousy, harboring unforgiveness, or failing to keep a promise. Or you may sense God's prompting to take an action but fail to follow through on it. Although the sins are not deliberate, your response is still from sinful human nature rather than the Holy Spirit.
> ➤ Sins of commission are intentional acts. You know your actions are wrong, yet you choose to move forward—regardless of the consequences. Galatians 5:19–21 provides some examples of intentional sins. Paul challenged the church at Galatia to live in ways that are holy and pleasing to God:

"Now the works of the flesh are evident: sexual immorality, impurity, sensuality, idolatry, sorcery, enmity,
strife, jealousy, fits of anger, rivalries, dissensions, divi-
sions, envy, drunkenness, orgies, and things like these.
I warn you, as I warned you before, that those who do
such things will not inherit the kingdom of God."

The term *works of the flesh,* also referred to as *sins of the flesh,* describes
sins you commit with your mind and body through the influence
of your soul. These are sins of commission. Notice Paul says these
sins are *evident*—an interesting word choice, which implies if you
commit any of these sins, you know you are doing something wrong.

Even though almost two thousand years have passed since Paul wrote
these words, the challenges we face in the twenty-first century are
similar. The works of the flesh, or sins of the flesh, are similar to the
lust of the flesh the apostle John divides into three categories:

"For everything in the world—the lust of the flesh,
the lust of the eyes, and the pride of life—comes not
from the Father but from the world. The world and
its desires pass away, but whoever does the will of God
lives forever" (1 John 2:16–17 NIV).

What is *the lust of the flesh?* This term refers to the use of your mind
and body in a sinful manner.

➤ *Sexual immorality, impurity, illicit sensualities.* Collectively,
these sins are carried out through your thoughts and physical actions and are illegal, and/or outside the boundaries of
biblical marriage (Genesis 2:24). This includes adultery, pornography, orgies, prostitution, or homosexuality. These sins

can also be manifested in an obsession with fantasy novels or other erotica that create sexual fantasies about someone other than your spouse.

Paul provides the right perspective on these sins in his first letter to the Corinthians:

"Flee from sexual immorality. Every other sin a person commits is outside the body, but the sexually immoral person sins against his own body. Or do you not know that your body is a temple of the Holy Spirit within you, whom you have from God? You are not your own, for you were bought with a price. So glorify God in your body" (1 Corinthians 6:18–20).

➤ *Drunkenness.* Intoxication through alcohol, prescription drugs, narcotics, or other faculty-altering substances which prevent you from living and thinking coherently.
➤ *Gluttony.* Greed or excessive eating, overspending (which can also lead to indebtedness), overdoing, and overindulging in anything that creates an unhealthy lifestyle and a perpetual focus on self-gratification (Philippians 3:18–19).

What is *the lust of the eyes?* This phrase refers to a desire to have someone who is not rightfully yours or something you mentally, emotionally, and physically do not own, earn, or deserve. Here are examples:

➤ *Greed.* The constant desire for more because you are never satisfied with what you have (Luke 12:15).
➤ *Stealing.* Taking something that is not yours from another person, organization, or group. This includes money,

possessions, or intellectual property, such as trade secrets or private information (Ephesians 4:28).

➤ *Abuse* (physical, sexual, verbal, and emotional). Rape, molestation, and murder fall into this category, as well as the lust of the flesh. You may associate these heinous crimes with sexual acts, but each also reflects a deliberate attempt to gain control over another human's life—or end it.

What is *the pride of life?* This attitude makes life all about you. It fosters emotions, thoughts, and actions that are self-serving and self-preserving at the expense of others:

➤ *Using God's name in vain.* Verbalizing the name of God, Jesus, or the Holy Spirit in a way that denigrates his sanctity, holiness, and sovereignty (Exodus 20:7).
➤ *Idolatry.* Making anything or anyone in your life more important than God.
➤ *Sorcery or witchcraft.* Black magic or casting evil spells on people and objects by calling on the spirits of darkness and their powers (2 Chronicles 33:6; Isaiah 8:19–20). You may wonder if this kind of evil is real. Yes, supernatural powers are genuine and should never be trivialized.
➤ *Enmity, strife, and fits of anger.* These emotions emerge from a deep place within you and are evidence of hostility and bitterness rooted and flourishing in your soul. Often directed toward another person, they stem from something done to you or said about you. Conflict and dysfunctional relationships can foster these destructive emotions.
➤ *Jealousy and envy.* An aggressive overprotection of your possessions and/or loved ones because of your unhealthy fear of loss. Jealousy develops when you wrongfully covet and become envious of what another person possesses.

➤ *Unhealthy rivalries.* Competitive behaviors that become unhealthy because of the deeply rooted desire to win and dominate another person, group, or team.

➤ *Dissension or division.* Disagreement leading to a condemning, harsh separation between two or more people.

➤ *Selfish ambition.* Putting your desires and actions above others' needs and interests. It includes using forms of manipulation to obtain what you want or putting others down to make yourself look better. Selfish ambition is similar to vain conceit and both are marked by excessive pride used as a weapon to dominate others for personal gain.

➤ *Lying and false testimony.* Intentionally deceiving or bearing false witness to protect yourself or gain something at the expense of others (Proverbs 19:5).

➤ *Revenge.* Seeking retaliation against someone because of a real or perceived hurt or wrong he or she has caused (Romans 12:17–21).

The Apostle James, the half-brother of Jesus, offers this counsel:

"Who is wise and understanding among you? By his good conduct let him show his works in the meekness of wisdom. But if you have bitter jealousy and selfish ambition in your hearts, do not boast and be false to the truth. This is not the wisdom that comes down from above, but is earthly [worldly], unspiritual, demonic. For where jealousy and selfish ambition exist, there will be disorder and every vile practice. But the wisdom from above is first pure, then peaceable, gentle, open to reason, full of mercy and good fruits, impartial and sincere. And a harvest of righteousness is sown in peace by those who make peace" (James 3:13–18).

## What Are Strongholds?

Strongholds are sins that control you. Like the chain that bound the elephant calf to the wood post, Satan uses strongholds to chain you to his control. You avoid additional pain when you submit to his control. But if you try to turn from the stronghold and start living right, all hell breaks loose. Exhausted, many cave to sin and give up hope. It's just too hard. The Enemy's grip subdues the fierce power of God, like the 12,000-pound elephant restrained by a thin rope.

Strongholds take myriad forms

- ➤ alcoholism and drug dependencies (narcotics or prescriptions)
- ➤ eating disorders (bulimia, anorexia)
- ➤ habitual use of and dependence on technology
- ➤ codependent relationships that feed on the attention and strength of others
- ➤ overindulgent behaviors such as spending, shopping, eating, working
- ➤ an uncontrollable sexual appetite that leads to illicit behaviors
- ➤ habitual condemnation, criticism, negativity, and fault-finding in others or yourself
- ➤ excessive lying and cheating
- ➤ untreated anxiety or depression
- ➤ a continual attempt to control others.

The Enemy may use many other kinds of ropes to entangle you. Stay on guard. Anything or anyone that draws you away from Jesus and your commitment to him can become a stronghold.

## What Are Idols?

In some countries, you can still find wooden idols carved by hand and offered for sale. In America, most people have traded carved images or idols for consuming careers, gargantuan homes, and luxurious automobiles. These sorts of idols strap us financially, but they may make us feel successful or enviable. Idols can also take the form of our actions, when we wear clothes that are too revealing, hold memberships we never use, and maintain schedules that are too full.

The works of the flesh and the bait that hooks you accentuate your pride by encouraging you to worship yourself or idols that make this life all about you. But God makes it clear in Exodus 20:4–6 he alone is to hold the central place in every person's life:

> "You shall not make for yourself a carved image, or any likeness of anything that is in heaven above, or that is in the earth beneath, or that is in the water under the earth. You shall not bow down to them or serve them, for I the LORD your God am a jealous God, visiting the iniquity of the fathers on the children to the third and the fourth generation of those who hate me, but showing steadfast love to thousands of those who love me and keep my commandments."

This second commandment (of the Ten Commandments) says do not *make for yourself a carved image*. A carved image is a god or idol to which people bow down in worship, believing the idol will answer questions, bring about prosperity, and give direction or protection.

If you own carved images, statues of religious saints, good luck charms, crystals, or other talismans, destroy them. Symbols of Buddhism, Taoism, or other forms of mystic religious idols and false gods have no place in the life of a follower of Jesus Christ. These objects, which may seem harmless, could give the Enemy a foothold in your life. Those who worship the dark spirits pray over these idols, which are physical items the second commandment warns against.

Ask God to reveal if any of your possessions represent an idol. Get rid of any evil influence.

## What Are Generational Curses?

You should also consider repetitious sins, with origins deeply rooted in your family. Is it a coincidence alcoholism, greed, sexual impropriety, and addictive patterns pass from generation to generation throughout various families and cultures? It may seem the children of these families face doom because of "inherited" behaviors from their father, mother, siblings, or extended family.

Exodus 20:5 references generational curses, or *iniquities of the father.* God allows consequences to affect children of the *third and the fourth generation* for the sins of those who worship idols rather than Jesus. The repetitious sins in your family could be a generational curse because your ancestors disregarded God's warning.

While the Enemy would like for you to believe you are a by-product of your family's generational choices and therefore doomed to repeat history, God is all powerful. He can set you free from these struggles so you will not pass generational curses down to your children and grandchildren.

## How Can You Be Separated from Sin?

In previous chapters, we defined sanctification as the lifelong process separating you from sin. Sanctification sets you free and makes your heart right with God. Through the Holy Spirit, Jesus works in and through you over time to change what you do with your soul and body. Jesus knows what chains Satan uses to pull you into his clutches. Jesus also sees the weakest areas (heart voids) within you.

As you take steps in your sanctification journey, do not feel discouraged when your flesh instinctively gravitates toward your weaknesses, sins, and strongholds. When you determine to offer your body as a living sacrifice and reprogram your mind (Romans 12:1–2), the Holy Spirit can complete his transforming work to separate you from the works of your flesh so you will be holy and pleasing to God.

Paul urges in 2 Corinthians 10:5, "We destroy arguments and every lofty opinion raised against the knowledge of God, and take every thought captive to obey Christ." Simply put, we should discuss our thoughts with Jesus to ensure we are not deceived by others. Sound difficult? At first it may feel that way, but just as you enjoy talking with your best friend, eventually you will find yourself talking to Jesus about everything. This intimate conversation prevents the Enemy from sidetracking you.

## When Are You Most Vulnerable to the Enemy?

A fish, like the marlin in Chapter 8, bites the baited hook because it appeals to him. Had I used different bait, I may not have caught the marlin. The Enemy knows the bait that most appeals to you.

Satan designs his bait for one purpose: to hook and drag you to spiritual death (John 10:10) by separating you from the peace of Jesus. You are vulnerable to Satan and evil when you allow sin to have dominion over you. But here's the good news: Jesus is greater than any temptation or sin you battle. He is stronger than any chain that holds you, and he can break any form of bondage that prevents you from walking in freedom—if you ask him to do so. Only Jesus can set you free from your bondage. He may choose to do it instantaneously or gradually.

The Apostle Paul counseled followers in Rome with this:

"So you also must consider yourselves dead to sin and
alive to God in Christ Jesus. Let not sin therefore reign
in your mortal body, to make you obey its passions.
Do not present your members to sin as instruments for

unrighteousness, but present yourselves to God as those who have been brought from death to life, and your members to God as instruments for righteousness. For sin will have no dominion over you, since you are not under law but under grace" (Roman 6:11–14).

Ask Jesus to reveal any sins or strongholds lurking in your heart. With his help and direction, healing and growth can occur. Choosing to fill your heart voids through selfish, sinful ambitions puts you on the wide path that leads to destruction. Walking the narrow path with Jesus through obedience leads to peace and rest. Come to Jesus and choose to change.

## Action Steps

1. Ask Jesus to reveal the sins you can't see and the strongholds where you struggle. How have these sins or strongholds affected you?

**2.** Read through the generational curses section. Thinking through your family history, list repetitious sins that cause you to struggle.

## Next Step on the Path

How do you live in peace rather than caught up in the world's chaos? Read Matthew 6:33–34 to prepare for the next chapter.

## Chapter Ten

# How Can I Find Peace?

Finding refuge from the impact of life's storms.

I ventured outside my home to assess the damage to our neighborhood. The ground was saturated. Giant oak trees uprooted. Rooftops were peeled back and debris covered the ground. It looked like a war zone. Three hurricanes had swept through Orlando in less than one month during 2004, destroying businesses, homes, structures, and greenways throughout central Florida. The eye of each storm had hovered over the city, creating an eerie but calming feeling. As I surveyed the damage and the sky, I realized I was standing underneath the third hurricane's eye, so I rushed back inside, knowing the backlash was coming.

Hurricanes form over water and can inflict catastrophic damage once they move inland. Even with modern meteorological technology to track the projected paths, nothing can prevent the storm.

The second hurricane that hit Florida in that month created several tornadoes. These funnel-shaped windstorms develop over land with little warning. The path of destruction is a visible alleyway, marked by the remnants of destroyed homes and buildings. On either side of the alleyway, other structures are untouched.

The word *storm* describes tumultuous life experiences, whether they are spiritual, mental, emotional, or physical. Like the destructive tornado, these events strike with a sharp, unexpected tragedy. Death, trauma, accidents, personal attacks, and job loss leave a trail of destruction like a tornado.

Other life storms hit like hurricanes. They brew well in advance, yet their monstrous impact is inescapable and their duration unknown. When we face defeating and abusive relationships, addiction or alcoholism, or the diagnosis of an incurable illness, it feels like a hurricane approaching from one direction, then hitting you from behind with another punch before you recover from the first blow.

Even if you intentionally seek a relationship with Jesus, you cannot avoid life's storms. But centering yourself in Jesus insulates you from their impact. How is this possible? The psalmist explained it this way:

> "Be merciful to me, O God, be merciful to me, for in
> you my soul takes refuge; in the shadow of your wings
> I will take refuge, till the storms of destruction pass by"
> (Psalm 57:1).

## In the Eye of the Storm

The eye, or center, of a storm is a serene place. The rapidly moving winds and debris of the tornado rip structures from their foundation, yet the air becomes strangely calm in the eye. Even while the winds and rain of a hurricane cause chaos and destruction, its center remains still—sometimes the sun may even shine.

Your journey with Jesus is like living in the calm center. Life's storms become strangely serene because your key focus becomes Jesus, not the storm. Consider the image Jesus used in Matthew 7:24–25.

"Everyone then who hears these words of mine and does them will be like a wise man who built his house on the rock. And the rain fell, and the floods came, and the winds blew and beat on that house, but it did not fall, because it had been founded on the rock."

Living presently in relationship with Jesus is a spiritual discipline. The core of your belief and trust in Jesus strengthens you so you can withstand the impact of inevitable storms. No matter how determined you are to live according to God's Word, when you depend on your mental and physical strength to survive, your body (flesh) and soul (mind, will, and emotions) become a target for Satan to strike repeatedly. The storm's circumstances weaken you. Remember, Satan knows the weaknesses which will lure you into old coping behaviors you've tried for mental and emotional support in the past. Jesus spoke about these ineffective barriers.

"And everyone who hears these words of mine and does not do them will be like a foolish man who built his house on the sand. And the rain fell, and the floods came, and the winds blew and beat against that house, and it fell, and great was the fall of it"
(Matthew 7:26–27).

Instead of seeing the situations as a threat to draw you away from Jesus and back into destructive patterns, consider them opportunities to become centered in his presence. In these storms, your trust in Jesus grows as you witness his ability to navigate you through them. Even in the most turbulent times, you can experience peace, joy, and hope:

"You make known to me the path of life; in your presence there is fullness of joy;

at your right hand are pleasures forevermore"
(Psalm 16:11).


## What Does Living in the Present Moment Look Like?

Stop. Close your eyes wherever you are at this moment and breathe in deeply. What do you hear? Feel? Smell? Think about the last time you slowed down and allowed yourself to experience the small pleasures of your five senses.

God created the heavens and the earth, "and God saw that it was good" (Genesis 1:12). How often do you look at creation and ponder its goodness? When did you last notice the intricate details of a flower or the granular veins of a leaf? Have you studied the never-ending sky at night from a dark, vacant field and marveled as the stars came to life, dancing and singing praise to their Creator? When was the last time you listened to the thunder roar, inhaled the freshness of an approaching storm, or danced in the rain? Have you ever praised God when you saw a rainbow as his symbol your troubles are ending?

Have you listened to the birds sing, the squirrels chatter as they search for food, or the trees whisper as their limbs sway in the evening breeze? Give yourself permission to pick up a stone and examine it. Skip your stone along a pond and watch its impact on the still waters. God invites you to rest. As the psalmist noted, "He makes me lie down in green pastures. He leads me beside still waters. He restores my soul. He leads me in paths of righteousness for his name's sake" (Psalm 23:2–3).

Put down your device. Smile at your neighbors. Listen attentively. Relish connections with others you might normally take for granted. Say with the psalmist, "This is the day that the LORD has made; let us rejoice and be glad in it" (Psalm 118:24).

Busyness steals the gift that living presently can unveil. Repeat the words from Psalm 16:11, "in your presence there is fullness of joy." Not in the past, nor the future. In the present, you experience Jesus and his character, the fruits of the Spirit, "love, joy, peace, patience, kindness, goodness, faithfulness, gentleness, self-control" (Galatians 5:22–23).

Even though you may lean into your walk with Jesus, you may find it difficult to rejoice if you are struggling against life's storms. Why? Your mental filters may have become clogged with life's debris, which can obstruct what God is doing in the present moment.

## Obstacles to Living in the Present: Past Pain, Future Fear

When you cannot see beyond your circumstances, you focus instead on the negative experiences and emotions—fear, doubt, and frustration. The Enemy uses these mental obstructions as part of his strategy.

Satan is a meticulous schemer, always attacking your vulnerability, pulling you back into past pain, paralyzing thoughts, and faulty reasoning. His schemes taint your present moments with confusion and doubt, fear and frustration. Like the back wall of a hurricane, the Enemy then launches another attack directed at the future and riddles you with fear of the unknown, attempting to squash your hopes and dreams. Your emotions continue to fuel this defeating circular motion until you cannot see a way out.

In chapter 1 we encounter Lory's story of abuse. For years her energy and emotions whirled from fear to anger to survival. Caught up in the constant churning, there was little time for thoughts of living presently. The cycle left Lory exhausted and vulnerable for the next attack. The Enemy used Lory's fear from past events to cast doubt on her future. The outcome appeared hopeless.

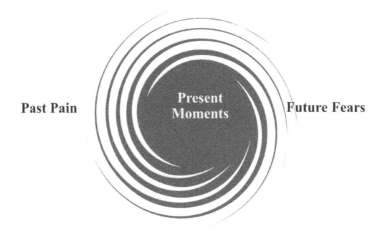

Past Pain     Present Moments     Future Fears

## How Do You Seek Jesus in the Present Moment?

Releasing the past and letting go of the future by intentionally living in the present is the only way to step out of this cyclical storm. How can you become centered in the present rather than *anxious* about life—"what you will eat or what you will drink, nor about your body, what you will put on" (Matthew 6:25)?

Caught in the cyclical storm within her home, Lory consciously chose salvation in Jesus and gave her circumstances to him. She took one day at a time and no longer focused on the anxiety surrounding tomorrow. She clung to the words of Jesus:

> "Seek first the kingdom of God and his righteousness, and all these things will be added to you. Therefore do not be anxious about tomorrow, for tomorrow will be anxious for itself. Sufficient for the day is its own trouble" (Matthew 6:33–34).

Jesus wants you to know he takes care of his creation, even "the birds of the air and the lilies of the field" (Matthew 6:26, 28). Using the simplistic lives of birds and lilies as examples, he points out they live without anxiety, glorifying God by living in the present moment. Jesus wants this simplicity for you.

Let's consider some actions steps for living presently.

**Be okay with yourself exactly as you are today.** Many of us dislike who and what we see in the mirror. Jesus sees past your imperfections, and he wants you to see yourself as he does. You are "fearfully and wonderfully made" (Psalm 139:14). The closer you draw to Jesus, the more he can cleanse your filters from sin, guilt, shame, pain, and fear.

**Peek into God's heart.** Throughout the Bible God uses unqualified and undesirable people—murderers, adulterers, liars, manipulators, idol worshipers, and others who have fallen—to complete his mighty work. This is proof that, once God grabs hold of a surrendered heart, anything is possible. Read God's Word as a love letter to you. Starting with the Psalms and the New Testament's letters of Paul, embrace the Bible as the personal story he is writing on your heart. Allow God to transform your thoughts like he did with the many who cried out to him to set their hearts free from the Enemy's chains of lies and despair.

**Praise God. Thank him often and lighten up.** When you develop the habit of watching for God's blessing and provision by *giving thanks in all circumstances,* God will draw you into present joy with him (1 Thessalonians 5:18). The Bible instructs you, as a follower of Jesus, to recognize and celebrate even the smallest blessing of God, because they ignite your passion and demonstrate your awe and reverence for him. Though sometimes we take our walk too seriously. God wants us to lighten up. Next time you recognize God's simplest touch, jump to your feet and slap a high five up to God, like a small child to his parent. Your heart will sing, and you'll probably put a smile on his face too.

**Live by faith, not by sight.** We human beings naturally put more confidence in what we see than in the faith God is developing within us. Following what is acceptable to the world allows the Enemy to influence you onto the wide path Jesus warned against (Matthew 7:13). For example, the world may tell us sex before marriage is okay. But our faith convicts us of the biblical truth which instructs us sex outside of marriage is sin.

Faith is "the assurance of things hoped for, the conviction of things not seen" (Hebrews 11:1). God has your best interest in mind in all circumstances, even when the action is difficult to do or contrary to what you see. If you step out in faith, God will place a deep knowing in your heart that continues to percolate until it becomes a conscious thought or action.

**Yoke yourself with Jesus.** A yoke is a wooden frame that joins two oxen together at the neck. These large animals work together to bear heavy loads and ensure one is not pulling more weight than the other. Jesus uses the metaphor of a yoke to help his followers understand the importance of connecting with him daily through relationship.

> "Come to me, all who labor and are heavy laden, and
> I will give you rest. Take my yoke upon you, and learn
> from me, for I am gentle and lowly in heart, and you
> will find rest for your souls. For my yoke is easy, and my
> burden is light" (Matthew 11:28–30).

Two yoked oxen are significantly stronger than one pulling a load alone. Jesus gives you *rest for your soul* so you can heal and think clearly in the present moment. Connecting yourself with Jesus matures your relationship with him, as he helps you carry your heavy burdens.

Circulating storms will continue, but the way you approach life changes when you live in the present moment with Jesus. He will cleanse your heart, removing the dark debris caused by sin and correcting the thought patterns and heart damage the world imposes on you. In these moments, you will find yourself in the center of his will, no longer struggling to withstand a storm's hurricane-force winds on your own, but resting in the calmness Jesus provides.

## Take Action

1. Re-read the section "What Does Living in the Present Moment Look Like" and engage one of the action steps to be still before God. Journal what you feel God put on your heart.

2. Write about a past pain or future fear that causes you anxiety. Now, working through the action steps outlined in this chapter, journal a "present moment" experience of releasing these anxieties to Jesus.

## Next Step on the Path

What does it mean to stand firm in life's battles? Read Ephesians 6:10–18 to prepare for the next chapter.

## Chapter Eleven

# How Can I Stand Firm in Life's Battles?

Countering spiritual attacks through God's Word.

Of all the places I've lived, Fayetteville, NC, was one of the most intriguing. Home of one of the largest military bases in the world, most of my neighbors and friends were military personnel, ranging from US Army Special Forces to Air Force Captains and an A-10 bomber fighter pilot. Listening to their conversations and war stories made neighborhood cookouts interesting.

The intelligence of these men and women struck me. Most of them spoke multiple languages and held college degrees far higher than the average citizen. Conversing with them gave me a deeper understanding of the strategic training they endure to protect their lives, defend our country, and fight confidently in battle. They must be prepared to stand firm, often with little or no notice. This is the same stance we must take in our battle against the Enemy.

# Prepare for Battle

As a follower in Christ, you will face battles "against enemy troops. Unlike the battles fought by armed forces, spiritual warfare is not waged against flesh and blood, but against the spiritual forces of evil" (Ephesians 6:12). Satan hates when you turn to Jesus for help. He will *attempt* to engage you in spiritual battles to keep you from walking in peace with Jesus. One of Satan's tactical plans is distraction. When you stroll along in the peace and light of Jesus, you may become complacent and forget that you are a constant target for Enemy attacks. But Jesus told his followers to be on guard.

> "I have told you these things, so that in me you may have peace. In this world you will have trouble. But take heart! I have overcome the world" (John 16:33 NIV).

Jesus states *you will have trouble*, but he does not want you to focus on the trouble as the Enemy wants you to do. Distractions cause you to fall into patterns of sin, and your Enemy will draw you back to the wide path.

Perhaps you have viewed your past spiritual battles as circumstantial or coincidental, recognizing only the hateful, discouraging, and manipulative actions of other people and attempting to remedy these situations in your strength. Satan orchestrates these circumstances. You must counter spiritual attacks with a spiritual weapon—God's Word.

In the book of Jude, the archangel Michael battled Satan. Although Michael was an angel and clearly empowered by God, he did not fight Satan in his strength. In verse 9, Michael countered Satan's threat through the power of God, stating, "The Lord rebuke you." Michael knew he was not powerful enough to overcome the evil forces of the Enemy. Neither are you. God alone is more powerful than Satan, and Satan must obey him.

To stand strong and remain protected against Satan, your heavenly Father gives you something more powerful, protective, and comprehensive than any military defensive strategy or gear: God's spiritual armor.

In Ephesians 6:10–19, the apostle Paul gives a clear description of the spiritual armor available to you for the "evil day" (ESV), or as another Bible version states, "when the day of evil comes" (v. 13 NIV):

> "Finally, be strong in the Lord and in the strength of his might. Put on the whole armor of God, that you may be able to stand against the schemes of the devil. For we do not wrestle against flesh and blood, but against the rulers, against the authorities, against the cosmic powers over this present darkness, against the spiritual forces of evil in the heavenly places. Therefore take up the whole armor of God, that you may be able to withstand in the evil day, and having done all, to stand firm. Stand therefore, having fastened on the belt of truth, and having put on the breastplate of righteousness, and, as shoes for your feet, having put on the readiness given by the gospel of peace. In all circumstances take up the shield of faith, with which you can extinguish all the flaming darts of the evil one; and take the helmet of salvation, and the sword of the Spirit, which is the word of God, praying at all times in the Spirit, with all prayer and supplication. To that end, keep alert with all perseverance, making supplication for all the saints."

This spiritual armor is not only for use during a life crisis or major catastrophe. Paul is also referring to the evil you may encounter every day. The Enemy usually attacks when you least expect an ambush and are most susceptible to distraction and sin.

Using the directives *put on* in verse 11 and *take up* in verse 13, Paul stresses that you, as a follower of Jesus, must take these actions if you are to successfully stand firm in your battles.

In verse 12, Paul clarifies you are not battling people, "flesh and blood," but "rulers, authorities, cosmic powers, present darkness, and spiritual forces of evil." Paul is likely referring to the legions of angelic beings (one third of the angels, according to Revelation 12:4) who fell from the Kingdom of God to serve Lucifer (Satan, the Devil). Ephesians 1:21 refers to these demons as a powerful army of evil. They have a threefold mission:

1) to destroy the church,
2) to prevent people from becoming followers of Christ, and
3) to prohibit Christians from walking in abundant life by stalemating their walk with Jesus.

To combat the Enemy and his army, clothe yourself in Jesus' attributes and carry your spiritual weaponry. Paul sandwiches our engagement in a spiritual war (verse 12) with the importance of wearing the *whole armor*. He knows victory comes from being prepared and wearing our armor every day.

## What Is the Armor of God?

In addition to the training and intelligence of my military friends, their combat uniforms were also impressive, each piece of their gear designed with intention and purpose. Specially constructed boots protect their feet and provide agility on various terrains. The belt holds reserve ammunition and combat weaponry. To protect the chest and vital organs, soldiers wear a ballistic vest with trauma plates. Their hard helmet deflects shrapnel and debris, and a mask or goggles prevent damage to their vision. A military-issued automatic rifle is attached by a strap and slung across their shoulder—readily accessible in case of an attack. Although battle gear weighs over ninety pounds, soldiers welcome its bulk because they know they are well protected.

God offers us this same sort of protection through our personalized suit of armor, designed for each believer by the Creator himself. This is what Paul impresses on the men and women of Ephesus when he tells them to "put on the whole armor of God." The reader in first-century Ephesus would have recognized the description of each piece of armor, based on the uniform Roman soldiers wore. Perhaps Paul wanted to emphasize the importance of preparing to stand strong in their spiritual battles just as the Roman soldiers trained and prepared for their physical battles.

Let's take it a step further and think of each piece of armor as a characteristic of Jesus uniquely designed to fit you perfectly, protecting you against evil assaults.

## The Belt of Truth

"Stand therefore, having fastened on the belt of truth" (Ephesians 6:14a). The belt of the Roman soldier's uniform fastened around his waist to gird and protect his midsection. But how can we spiritually wrap ourselves in truth?

Truth is a fact that never changes. Stand up and drop a pencil. You know gravity causes it to fall to the ground. Gravity is truth. In this ever-wavering society of false doctrine and irreligious beliefs, truth brings consistency and stability to your life. Jesus is "the way, the *truth,* and the life" (John 14:6). And this truth is your spiritual foundation.

Without abdominal muscles wrapped around your physical core, your body cannot stand erect. Without the biblical *truth* of God wrapped around your spiritual core, you cannot stand upright before the Enemy. The belt of truth guards you against the deception and schemes of the Enemy, "for he is a liar and the father of lies" (John 8:44).

## The Breastplate of Righteousness

"And having put on the breastplate of righteousness" (Ephesians 6:14b). Just as the breastplate protected the Roman soldier's heart and other vital organs, the breastplate of righteousness protects your spiritual heart.

The modern-day soldier's breastplate deflects shrapnel. A baseball catcher's chest-protector softens the blow from a fastball. The righteousness of Jesus shields you when the Enemy launches his evil attack. Only Jesus was perfect, righteous, and sinless. His sacrifice on the cross was an act of love providing you his righteousness when you are faithful and obedient. "But since we belong to the day, let us be sober, having put on the breastplate of faith and love, and for a helmet the hope of salvation" (1 Thessalonians 5:8).

## The Shoes of Peace

"And, as shoes for your feet, having put on the readiness given by the gospel of peace" (Ephesians 6:15). Paul illustrates peace as a pair of shoes, the firm foundation from which you step forward in the "gospel of peace" and fight every battle. Roman soldiers in Paul's time wore sandals that laced up the lower leg and covered their shins with brass. Their soles were trimmed with nails, giving them traction to stand firm in battle. Practical for battle, but likely not comfortable.

Nothing is better than a great pair of shoes, comfortably broken in for work, a good run or night out with friends. But you cannot break shoes in unless you wear them repeatedly, over time. Spending time in God's Word and the loving presence of Jesus helps you stand firm in the knowledge he loves and protects you. God's peace covers you, regardless of the outcome of your earthly battles.

## The Shield of Faith

"In all circumstances take up the shield of faith, with which you can extinguish all the flaming darts of the evil one" (Ephesians 6:16).

When skillfully positioned in battle, the Roman soldier's shield protected him from enemy weaponry. Your shield of faith represents absolute trust in the power of Jesus to "extinguish all the flaming darts of the evil one." Satan targets your heart with sinful temptations, distracting thoughts, and doubt.

As a Marvel's Avengers fan, I picture my faith as Captain America's shield. Your faith shield allows you to stand firm, knowing faith is "the assurance of things hoped for, the conviction of things not seen" (Hebrews 11:1). But even Captain America needed practice learning to brandish his shield against enemy attacks.

When Satan casts doubt that God loves you, for example, consciously recall the times he's rescued you from sin and pain. Utilizing Jesus' authority to recognize the Enemy's attacks against your weakness takes time and spiritual training. As your confidence grows, the shield *of faith* extinguishes these darts *before* they enter your mind, when you take all thoughts captive to Jesus. Both Old Testament and New Testament writers affirm, "the righteous shall live by faith."[3]

## The Helmet of Salvation

"And take the helmet of salvation" (Ephesians 6:17a). Next, Paul encourages you to protect your mind as a follower of Jesus.

On the gridiron, football players must wear helmets to survive head-on collisions with opponents. Paul's reference to the *helmet of salvation* emphasizes the critical importance of safeguarding your mental transformation from the Enemy. Satan wants you to doubt your eternal salvation, the hope you have in Jesus (Romans 12:2). He wants you to think you are worthless, undeserving.

Putting on your helmet, the knowledge of your salvation through Jesus which no one can take from you, will strengthen you. It protects your soul—mind, will, and emotions—as you grow stronger in your

[3] See Habakkuk 2:4, Romans 1:17, Galatians 3:11, and Hebrews 10:38.

faith. Surrounded by enemies, David wrote, "But you, O LORD, are a shield about me, my glory, and the lifter of my head" (Psalm 3:3).

## The Sword of the Spirit

"And the sword of the Spirit, which is the word of God" (Ephesians 6:17b). Paul depicts the sixth piece of armor differently from all the others. The belt of truth, breastplate of righteousness, shoes for your feet, shield of faith, and helmet of salvation are defensive pieces of armor. The Word of God, however, is your one piece of offensive weaponry. "For the word of God is living and active, sharper than any two-edged sword" (Hebrews 4:12a).

Attempting to defeat the Enemy without the Word of God is the same as a soldier entering battle without his weapon. But how do you learn to wield the sword of the Spirit like a *two-edged sword* rather than a butter knife?

Your spiritual sword's effectiveness is in direct proportion to your closeness with Jesus. As you read, study, and mature in understanding his Word, your ability to wield your weapon and strike blows will increase. Of course, expertise requires practice, so keep in mind that "walking" with Jesus is a marathon, not a sprint. Recite verses and sing them in praise songs.

In Matthew 4:1-11, Jesus used the Word of God to fend off Satan. Jesus internalized the Word, making it a part of him and allowing the Spirit to move through it. By focusing on God's Word and allowing it to saturate your soul, the movement of your sword becomes as skillful as a ninja swinging his sword, defeating his foes. The Enemy will flee, for he fears the invincible Word of God.

"Submit yourselves therefore to God. Resist the devil,
and he will flee from you. Draw near to God, and he
will draw near to you" (James 4:7–8).

## How Do You Stand Firm in Your Armor?

In Ephesians 6, Paul shares the importance of standing firm in your battles three times.

➤ *"Put on the whole armor of God, that you may be able to stand against the schemes of the devil" (vs. 11)*
➤ *"And having done all, to stand firm" (vs. 13)*
➤ *"Stand therefore" (vs. 14)*

What does Paul mean when he tells us to stand? Have confidence (faith) in the truth of God's Word. Standing strong is key to our victory against evil. When we understand Jesus has already won the victory at the cross, we realize our spiritual battles are not fought to gain victory but from a place of victory.

This knowledge empowers us to stand strong on his promises, engage the Word as our sword, and combat the Enemy's lies and deception. As Moses told the Israelites at the Red Sea, "The LORD will fight for you, and you have only to be silent" (Exodus 14:14).

Suppose a woman who frequently struggles with anxiety and depression is waiting for a health prognosis. Aware of her weakness, the Enemy prods her with endless worst-case scenarios. Her fear and anxiety morph into depression as the Enemy's taunts lead her down the path she's traveled so often.

As she slips into the depression, she puts on her spiritual armor. First, she grabs the *belt of truth* by allowing the Holy Spirit to remind her of what she read recently in her Bible. (As a follower, you soon learn that there are no coincidences with God, only God-incidences.) With hope, she picks up the *sword of the Spirit* and turns to Philippians 4:6–7, "Do not be anxious about anything, but in everything by prayer and supplication with thanksgiving let your requests be made known to God. And the peace of God, which surpasses all understanding, will guard your hearts and your minds in Christ Jesus."

She wields the *sword of the Spirit*, reciting the Philippians passage over and over. Although it seems difficult—maybe even silly—at first, she talks to Jesus aloud about her health prognosis. She thanks the Holy Spirit for reminding her of the verses in Philippians and tells him about the anxiety she is feeling. To deflect the Enemy's flaming darts, she lifts her *shield of faith* and recites the Scripture out loud, more boldly.

Her focus shifts from mounting fear and depression to Jesus. Donning the *helmet of salvation*, she surrenders the outcome to him because she trusts him with her circumstances. She stands firm in her *shoes of peace*. Her crisis has not changed, but the way she views them has. Through the truth and righteousness given to her in Jesus Christ, she knows that the *breastplate of righteousness* guarded her heart and mind from the Enemy's attack.

Like this woman, you can remain confident that by the power and blood of Jesus, you can overcome the Enemy's attack by standing firm in your armor, by being "strong in the Lord and in the strength of his might" (Ephesians 6:10). This is the strength that raised Jesus from the dead. Knowing this, is there anything God cannot walk you through?

As my military friends know, the threat of warfare for our country is constant and tangible. Our armed forces must remain armed and prepared. Their vigilance inspires me to stand firm in my spiritual battles. I know I am already victorious in Christ because he conquered Satan and death at the cross. But only by clothing myself in the attributes of Jesus—the whole armor of God—can I successfully stand strong against evil. If you put on your spiritual armor each day, you can stand strong against the Enemy's attacks too.

## Take Action

**1.** Think of a recent circumstance in which you found yourself defeated by spiritual warfare. Now, envision putting on the armor of God one piece at a time, as if you are dressing for the day. Walk through the situation utilizing the power of each piece. How could you have approached the situation from a place of victory rather than fighting for victory?

**2.** What do you consider your greatest weakness—the place where Satan attacks you most? Ask God for scripture that counters your weakness. Recite and memorize it. Wield your sword in moments of Enemy attack. Stand firm and believe you will be victorious.

## Next Step on the Path

How can you open your heart to a relationship with Jesus? Read Hosea 10:12 from the New Living Translation to prepare for the next chapter.

# PART THREE

# Understanding Yourself

"Let us draw near to God with a sincere heart and with
the full assurance that faith brings, having our hearts
sprinkled to cleanse us from a guilty conscience and
having our bodies washed with pure water"
(Hebrews 10:22 NIV)

*Chapter Twelve*

# What Does It Mean to Seek Jesus?

Opening our hearts to God positions us to
experience his infinite blessings.

A long drought hardened the ground at the ranch. I tapped the
surface with my shovel. Dense as concrete. The only tool that
could penetrate the soil was an unstable 1954 Allis Chalmers tractor
with an augur attached. I thought if I put my full weight on the auger,
I could force it into a side-to-side grinding motion that would break
up the ground while the tractor operator tried to control the rig. We
tackled the task with tenacity and perseverance, slowly turning the
soil one post-hole at a time.

Like that compacted soil, our heart can harden without the nutrient
of unconditional love. In this impenetrable state, we cannot receive
the mental, emotional, spiritual, or even physical healing Jesus
provides.

The heart represents all that you are—spirit, soul, body and personality. The prophet Hosea gives further insight about what God desires of your heart.

"Plow up the hard ground of your hearts, for now is the time to seek the LORD, that he may come and shower righteousness upon you" (Hosea 10:12b NLT).

Hosea highlights three important elements. Two of them require our action—*plow up the hard ground of your hearts* and *seek the LORD*. The third element—*that he may come and shower righteousness upon you*—is what God does when you act on the first two requirements.

## Your Part: Step #1

*Plow up the hard ground of your heart.* Perhaps taking this first step is easier than it seems. When I first dug into the hardened soil at the ranch, the task seemed impossible, but time and effort proved the job was possible. If God prompts you to do something, he will enable you to do it. He desires to free the human heart from the bondage of sin, so he makes a way.

The first step in breaking up the hardness of your heart is opening your heart to Jesus. Talk to him about past or present situations that have caused pain, sorrow, defeat, failure, and other debilitating feelings. Healing in the heart comes from first exposing the pain to Jesus.

Opening our heart to Jesus can elicit deep emotions and what-ifs, especially if we've endured intense pain or failure.

➤ *Fear.* What if someone hurts me again?
➤ *Remorse.* What if God is ashamed of me?

- *Apprehension.* What will happen to me if I give up control?
- *Self-Condemnation.* What if this *is all my fault?*

Two elements fuel these emotions: *condemnation* or *conviction.* The Enemy condemns. God convicts.

Condemnation comes from self-imposed thoughts or external influences that create feelings of shame, unworthiness, or defectiveness. Think of condemnation as an internal bully who tries to press you down. Every time you try to rise, the bully points out unworthiness, repeated mistakes, shame, and failures. He attempts to instill doubt of ever changing or moving beyond your current circumstances. This internal bully is the Enemy described in John 10:10. His purpose is to destroy your purpose and belief that your life is worth anything.

God's conviction results from sin you committed or are about to commit. He knows sin damages your relationship with Jesus and separates you from him. Conviction is God's gift to correct and protect you from destruction and the bondage of sin.

Understanding the difference between condemnation and conviction is critical. You need to recognize the difference between the bully's voice (the Enemy's) and God's voice. The Enemy's goal is to tempt and mislead you. God desires to breathe new life into your body and soul through his Spirit.

Conviction manifests in various ways:

- A quiet voice (God's voice) within the soul.
- "Coincidental" external circumstances.
- A scripture, devotion or podcast.
- A sense of heaviness that won't let up after a failure.

What happens once conviction brings sin or a sense of unsettledness to mind? God's prompting encourages you to bring specific issues to Jesus so he can release you from unhealthy habits or thought patterns.

Fear of failure—or even of success—unforgiveness, lustful thoughts, pain, addictions, lying, greed, or other repetitive acts that result in cycles of unhealthy emotions can harden your heart.

Come clean and restore your relationship with Jesus by repenting, which means to confess and then turn away from sin and poor choices.

"For godly grief produces a repentance that leads to salvation without regret, whereas worldly grief produces death" (2 Corinthians 7:10).

As you bring baggage, faults, and failures to Jesus, say something like this:

*Jesus, thank you for allowing me to come to you just the way I am. I lay my fears and failures, my hurts and sorrows, my past and present before you. Please help me sift through the emotions and experiences that have hardened my heart. Grant me wisdom to understand how these thoughts and actions have created a barrier between us. I ask for your forgiveness. Help me forgive myself. In your name, I pray. Amen.*

Jesus sometimes provides instant healing. Other times, he heals gradually. But he is always listening (1 Peter 3:12). To *plow up the hard ground of your heart,* allow him to bring healing to the heart voids, whether these voids have recently occurred or have been years in the making. Your part is to come to him with what he places on your heart and mind through conviction.

A surrendered, repentant heart becomes pliable in Jesus' hands, as he reshapes and restores it. He has promised, "And I will give you a new heart, and a new spirit I will put within you. And I will remove the heart of stone from your flesh and give you a heart of flesh" (Ezekiel 36:26).

**Your Part: Step #2**

*Seek the Lord.* How do you seek Jesus when he is not visible? You cannot touch him or match his power. Faith is the key to seeking and walking with Jesus. Faith affects how you think, believe, and live with exuberant passion for Jesus. By faith, seek Jesus and learn to "love the Lord your God with all your heart and with all your soul and with all your mind and with all your strength" (Mark 12:30).

How is it possible to love God this way? Seek him.

➤ Spend intentional time alone with God at a park or on a walk, taking in the silence and observing his creation.

➤ Read the Bible and talk to Jesus about what you are learning. Ask him questions and listen as he leads you to the answers.

➤ Journal what Jesus reveals. Keep a continuous diary of your relationship with him.

➤ Fellowship with other people who believe in Jesus to grow in relationship with him together.

➤ Worship Jesus by listening to praise music. Sing songs with gusto, alone or in a group.

➤ Thank Jesus—frequently. Recognize his role in both the big and small blessings of life, and thank him for what he is doing.

➤ Remember to talk to Jesus throughout the day—nothing is too small or too big to discuss with him. Frequent communication fine-tunes your spiritual ear to hear him when he speaks.

Simply put, Jesus wants you to seek him with every part of your being and every aspect of your life. Pursuing him takes time and intentionality. Relationships grow when two people put forth effort to know each another. A relationship with Jesus is no different. In seeking Jesus, you begin to understand the complexity of the heart.

## God's Part: The Yield

God tells us to plow up the hardness of our heart by opening our heart to Jesus and by seeking him with our entire being. What is the result—the yield—of our commitment? When you and I pursue Jesus with tenacity and perseverance, God responds by pouring his righteousness on, in, and through us.

To be righteous is to be morally right. Who can live up to such a high standard? Maybe judges or clergy? The Bible declares emphatically, "None is righteous, no, not one" (Romans 3:10).

No human is righteous. You and I still battle sin even after we've given our hearts to Jesus. How, then, can we ever experience freedom from sin if we are not "right*eous*"?

Righteousness defines Jesus, the Son of God. He is holy—without sin. He embodies the message of grace and mercy. He is the ultimate example of moral rightness and justice. Jesus, therefore, is the only one who can redeem us from our sins. He is the island of justice in the ocean of our chaotic culture.

Through our relationship with Jesus, we receive his gifts of grace and mercy. Grace is tenderness and kindness, which we do not deserve. God gives grace as a gift with no strings attached. His generous grace frees us from the penalty of sin (death) and offers the ultimate gift of eternity (life) with God.

Mercy is God's compassion and favor because he knows we are only human. At its core, mercy is forgiveness. He shows us mercy by blessing and forgiving us and leading us to a better way to live.

We categorize sins. We consider some bad, but others are horrific. For example, we may consider murder a horrendous sin, but lying a mistake or minor sin. In God's eyes, sin is sin.

King David committed adultery, followed by premeditated murder. David's failure was horrendous. His poor choices and evil actions brought this strong and mighty man of God to one of the lowest points of his life. As rich and as powerful as David was, all he could offer God was remorse. In Psalm 51, David repents, "The sacrifices of God are a broken spirit; a broken and contrite heart, O God, you will not despise" (v. 17). He approached God with a heart that was *contrite*, which means "remorseful" and "in a state of repentance."

All sin separates us from God, which is why he wants us to come to him as David did—with a repentant, humbled heart. We cannot earn grace or mercy. We can only experience these gifts with Jesus, as he covers us in his righteousness.

## Jesus' Part: The Living Water

God immediately begins cultivating your heart once you open it to him. He pours his Spirit into your spirit, to reveal his presence, holiness, healing and guidance. Think of his outpouring as water flowing from heaven, like a mountain river, pure and clear.

The powerful rush of cool, clean water dislodges debris in a riverbed. The living waters of Jesus cleanse the impurities from your cultivated heart. As Jesus saturates you, the riverbed of your heart becomes wide and deep to increase the flow of water to a destination further downstream.

"If anyone thirsts, let him come to me [Jesus] and
drink. Whoever believes in me, as the Scripture has said,
'Out of his heart will flow rivers of living water'"
(John 7:37–38).

Jesus fills your heart with spiritual living water—his righteousness.
As it flows through, it touches the lives of others and draws them to
him.

The tractor operator and I set sixteen posts in the hardened soil
that day. Although my body ached and we were exhausted, we
accomplished the impossible task of plowing up the ground because
we intentionally persevered. Hosea 10:12 beckons you to allow
Jesus to plow up that hardened ground of your heart. Jesus said "the
way is hard that leads to life" because he knows difficult times are
unavoidable (Matthew 7:14). As you seek Jesus with intentionality
and perseverance, he showers you with living waters of righteousness
and healing.

## Take Action

**1.** Express to God—aloud or on paper—feelings, thoughts, sins,
or weaknesses you have never been able to talk to him about.

**2.** Journal an action plan to engage Your Part, Step #1 and #2 as they are defined in the chapter.

## Next Step on the Path

Can Jesus really change you? Prepare for chapter 13 by reading Romans 12:1–2.

*Chapter Thirteen*

# Can Jesus Help Me Change?

God speaks clearly through the works of his creation.

As I entered the tropical habitat of the Butterfly Garden in St. Thomas, Virgin Islands, spectacular colors and shapes of tiny, winged creatures filled the air around me. Species from every continent brushed my skin as they fluttered past. Each butterfly was living proof of the unlimited imagination of our Creator.

Curiosity drew me to the educational exhibit chronicling the butterfly's metamorphosis. I studied the tiny egg that would advance to the caterpillars I saw hungrily eating the vegetation around them. I marveled at the chrysalises attached to leaves, molting from one stage of growth to the next. As I bent to listen closely, the trembling wings inside the protective casing created a faint but musical sound. Only God can do this, I thought.

Imagine the time and attention God chose to spend on the tiny details of this creature. If he loves the butterfly this much, how much more did he enjoy creating each of us? Watching us grow from birth to adulthood. The butterfly's metamorphosis to a changed creature reminds me God also nurtures the transformation in us spiritually.

## The Stages of Spiritual Metamorphosis

Our spiritual transformation begins when we admit our need for a Savior and ask Jesus to forgive our sins. Our salvation is distinct and immediate—and the deepest personal experience. But our walk to live out who we are as a new person in Christ is a lifelong journey. The Apostle Paul writes about this process when he says, "Work out your own salvation with fear and trembling, for it is God who works in you, both to will and to work for his good pleasure" (Philippians 2:12b–13).

New followers of Jesus are in the caterpillar stage. You have experienced a new birth, and, like the hungry caterpillar, growth occurs by devouring everything God reveals. You study the Bible, read devotions, attend classes, and associate with others who know and love Jesus. In this stage, spiritual maturity develops through a better understanding of how to walk alongside Jesus on the narrow path with intentionality and perseverance. As the relationship with God deepens, you learn to listen for his voice and become excited watching his will unfold.

Seasoned Christians experience the chrysalis stage of metamorphosis. The caterpillar molts from one form to the next as a chrysalis, which many believe is a time of inactivity for the butterfly. But big changes are happening—cells grow, eyes appear and wings begin to sprout. As Christians change by absorbing God's love and wisdom, they reflect the nature of Jesus. In this exciting stage, God continues to build a spiritual stamina so followers can persevere through the journey.

Throughout these stages, we must be open to the work God is doing in our hearts. As he peels away layers of guilt, shame, pain, misunderstanding, or fear, we may be surprised. Spiritual surgery, or sanctification, is necessary to reveal the nucleus of who we are in Christ.

Jesus has the supernatural ability to change us from who we used to be to a *new creation,* completely free and transformed into his image. "Therefore, if anyone is in Christ, he is a new creation. The old has passed away; behold, the new has come" (2 Corinthians 5:17). Why is change so critical? Because the Enemy peppers us with reminders of failures and sin, attempting to lead us away from Jesus. We can defend against his attacks by remembering we became a new creation in Christ when we gave him our heart. The old life has passed away, and the new life has come. Watch with gratitude and wonder as he transforms spirit, soul, and body to walk in ways that are holy and pleasing to him.

Jesus brings about spiritual metamorphosis through a gradual progression from a newborn Christian (larva) to an adult Christian (butterfly). Two questions based on Romans 12:1–2 help us understand how Jesus transforms us.

"Therefore, I urge you, brothers and sisters, in view of God's mercy, to offer your bodies as a living sacrifice, holy and pleasing to God—this is your true and proper worship" (NIV)

## Question #1: Are You Honoring God with Your Body?

The Apostle Paul wrote the book of Romans as a letter to those who are a part of God's Christian Church[4] and family. Paul uses a strong verb, *urge,* to get their attention and to emphasize the importance of his words, "offer your bodies as a living sacrifice."

We should also take his words seriously. But the metaphor he uses— living sacrifice—may be unfamiliar to us. How can we translate Paul's

[4] Church, when capitalized, refers to the Christian Church in general: the entire body of Christ, all those who believe in Jesus as Savior.

message into today's language?

To properly interpret a biblical text and apply God's Word, we first research the historical context of the writing. Many study Bibles offer historical background for each book of the Bible, detailing the approximate date written, the historical background of the author, and the region in which the book was written. Biblical cultures were different from our society today. If we study the time-period of the writing and the author's original purpose, we can understand the author's intent.

The original readers of Paul's urgent message would have understood his analogy. God required the Jewish priests who served during the Old Testament period to offer unblemished animal sacrifices as burnt offerings for the atonement (forgiveness) of sins for the Jewish people. Animal sacrifices were no longer necessary following the death of Jesus on the cross. Why? Because Jesus was the perfect sacrificial lamb, unblemished and without sin (Hebrews 4:15). God sent Jesus as the substitute to pay the penalty for sin: "He is the propitiation for our sins, and not for ours only but also for the sins of the whole world" (1 John 2:2).

Paul is not suggesting his readers offer their bodies as sacrifices on a stone altar. Paul uses the word *sacrifice* symbolically, imploring us to adopt and maintain a sacrificial lifestyle and to use our body to serve the Lord, not ourselves.

Another key point in Paul's message here is the phrase, *in view of God's mercy*. What does God desire from his followers? He wants us to come to him with a humble, contrite heart and respond to his mercy with obedience and faithfulness. He created us to enjoy the abundance of walking in his will. Paul describes our journey with God in Romans 12:1 as "true and proper worship."

## Question #2: Who Directs Your Thought Life—the World or Jesus?

"Do not conform to the pattern of this world, but be transformed by the renewing of your mind. Then you will be able to test and approve what God's will is—his good, pleasing and perfect will" (Romans 12:2 NIV).

In verse two, Paul continues his sense of urgency and direction. First, he charged us to no longer *conform to the pattern of this world.* 'World' in the New Testament is usually the Greek word *kosmos,* meaning order. When God created the universe and mankind, he set the wheels in motion for the stars and planets to move in orbits, and he embellished all the universe with beauty.

But the world as we know it is under the power of Satan, "the evil one" (1 John 5:19). His influence over the world paved the wide path that leads many to destruction (Matthew 7:13). Paul warns against this path when he refers to the *pattern of this world.* The *pattern* consists of the habits, beliefs, and lifestyles that lead people away from Jesus and toward the love of self and the world.

It is impossible to love what is in the world and love God at the same time. God blesses us through the joys of family and friends, careers, hobbies, and even possessions. But we must resist the urge to love people and things as idols—any item or person more important than God. The Bible warns against affection for this world and all that is in it. "Do not love the world or anything in the world. If anyone loves the world, love for the Father is not in them" (1 John 2:15 NIV).

Things of the world have a tendency to ignite lustful pleasures (1 John 2:16-17). When we lust, we desire to have a pleasure or a person now. Lust wants more and drives us toward cravings to satisfy the desires of the flesh.

Jesus transforms our mind through renewal. Think of the metamorphosis of the caterpillar molting one outer layer at a time. Each layer reveals a transformed creature, waiting for the next stage. We shed habits and beliefs formed prior to salvation when they do not line up with the truth of God's Word. To have lasting heart change, we first undergo a head change—our mind. When our mind changes, we are influenced more by our spirit and less by our flesh. We will continue to discard worldly influences. Our thoughts will circle back to Jesus and his Word. Here's how the apostle Paul explains it:

"If then you have been raised with Christ, seek the things that are above, where Christ is, seated at the right hand of God. Set your minds on things that are above, not on things that are on earth. For you have died, [to self] and your life is hidden with Christ in God. When Christ who is your life appears, then you also will appear with him in glory. Put to death therefore what is earthly [worldly] in you: sexual immorality, impurity, passion, evil desire, and covetousness, which is idolatry" (Colossians 3:1–5).

As we keep our mind on Jesus, the choices we make regarding our physical body change. The cravings of our flesh weaken. What brought temporal pleasure and satisfied cravings no longer fulfills us. The sin that used to excite us now generates pain, guilt, and shame.

Even as we develop a more intimate relationship with Jesus, earthly pleasures will attract our body and mind. Continue to seek Jesus. Taking all thoughts to Jesus in prayer forms a habit of dialogue and shifts our mind from focusing on the world to focusing on our desire of faithfulness to him (2 Corinthians 10:5).

In this way, Jesus changes, or transforms us.

## How Do You Steer Your Focus?

Have you ever watched a NASCAR or IndyCar driver run into the wall as he enters a turn, even when no other cars are nearby? One-car crashes occur because of the driver's focus—on the wall. Successful racecar drivers must learn to navigate turns. The angle of a curve and the rate of speed can be deceiving if the driver is not prepared to maneuver through the turn with absolute concentration. A driver knows where he focuses his gaze is where his car will end up. Instructors teach the driver to focus on the darkened pavement when entering a turn, as it indicates the trajectory other drivers have successfully navigated. Therefore, if a driver looks at the wall, instead of the darkened pavement, his car will follow his line of sight into the wall.

This principle applies to our walk with Jesus. If we focus our line of sight on sin, desires, and worldly influences, we will eventually hit a wall. We'll swerve onto the wide, destructive path again and again. We can only break this pattern by taking control of thoughts—bring them to Jesus and allow him to transform our mind.

Timing is everything. On a recent family trip, our teenage son learned a valuable lesson about timing in heavy highway traffic. Traveling at the recommended speed, he saw cars in front of him slam on the brakes. He had a fraction of a second to do the same and managed to avoid a major accident. You and I have a split second to filter the decisions and thoughts that enter our mind.

Although God is transforming our soul through sanctification, parts of our soul still wander toward the wide path, delighting in sins, habits, or unhealthy self-image. In these cases, we need to make a quick decision. Entertain these thoughts and allow our mind to go there? Or take these thoughts immediately to Jesus? God does not tempt us with thoughts of negative self-image or sinful flirtation. These thoughts are either from the Enemy or from the unsanctified part of our soul.

No matter how tempting thoughts may be, if we listen to Jesus, he will always show the way out:

> "No temptation has overtaken you that is not common to man. God is faithful, and he will not let you be tempted beyond your ability, but with the temptation he will also provide the way of escape, that you may be able to endure it" (1 Corinthians 10:13).

Thoughts holy and pleasing to God produce righteous living. As God transforms our soul, thoughts coming from him allow us to make the right choices. We cannot let down our guard because the Enemy doesn't stop. Sound exhausting, maybe even impossible?

In chapter eight, I shared a simple exercise to help develop the habit of taking thoughts to Jesus. Hold your hand up with your fingers spread out. As thoughts come to you, symbolically grab the thought with your hand by clenching your fist. Next, discuss with Jesus the thought in your clenched fist. Is the thought healthy and positive? If so, hold onto it. If the thought is destructive, ask Jesus to discard it. Keep the good thoughts, and, with a hand gesture, toss the negative ones away. It may be helpful to say aloud, "I'll have no more of this … because I am a new person in Christ."

During the search for a new family home, Lory and I quickly learned we were in a chaotic seller's market with low home inventory in the area we desired. What started as a joy-filled expedition became stressful and disappointing. We lifted our discouragement to God in prayer. Grasping the negativity, we asked God to replace the chaos with peace. Soon our excitement returned.

Changing our thought patterns requires energy and intentionality. Transformational change comes from Jesus as a result of our faithfulness to him—taking captive every thought to make it obedient to Christ. Acknowledging the work Jesus has done in us creates humility. And a humble heart is a heart Jesus can transform.

## How Do You Deal with Failure?

You are human and will not always capture thoughts in time to make them obedient to Jesus. When you fall prey to thoughts leading into temptation and sin, repent and ask Jesus for forgiveness. But don't assume you can sin all you want, knowing that Jesus will forgive you. The man who leaves his wife for another woman may say, "After I do this, I'll ask God's forgiveness." This trick is the Enemy's scheme to lead you to the wide path.

God is less concerned about your track record, however, than he is about a humble heart. God desires you grow closer to him, fall more in love with him. He is not concerned about you becoming religious or pursuing perfection. He wants you to become holy, seeking him even when you fail. Stop focusing on spiritual successes or failures and focus on Jesus.

Find a Bible that highlights Jesus' words in red print throughout the four Gospels. Imagine you are in the story with Jesus and he is speaking directly to you. Look into his eyes as he smiles at you. Sit across from him at the table and listen to him teach. Walk with Jesus and the other disciples on dusty roads. Step into his story and out of yours so Jesus can transform your mind.

## Can Jesus Transform You?

I believe God created the butterfly to remind us transformation into a beautiful, grace-filled creature is possible. Approach your relationship with the knowledge that "he must increase, but I must decrease" (John 3:30). The Bible reveals "you will be able to test and approve what God's will is—his good, pleasing and perfect will" (Romans 12:2 NIV). Through sanctification, you become less of self and more of Jesus. And permanent spiritual change allows you to become God's beautiful, unique creation, flying free in grace.

## Take Action

**1.** In your journal, describe the stages of your spiritual growth—from where you began to where Jesus has brought you today.

**2.** What challenges you most—honoring God with your body? Taking your thoughts captive to Jesus? Write your struggles in your journal asking Jesus why they remain such a challenge.

## Next Step on the Path

How do you know if you are really surrendered to Jesus? Read Psalm 37:4 to get a glimpse of the surrendered heart of a follower of Jesus.

## Chapter Fourteen

# How Can I Take a Leap of Faith?

**Surrender means giving up our control to experience all of Jesus.**

I couldn't catch my breath. Falling at 120 miles per hour, the crushing sensation felt like bricks on my chest trapping the air deep in my lungs. Gulping one conscious breath at a time, composure replaced panic on a thrilling thirteen-thousand-foot tandem parachute jump.

The moment we pushed through the yawning mouth of the plane the roaring wind drowned out the heartbeat slamming in my ears. I was grateful for the securely clamped harness connecting me to my instructor, a passionate military professional with 4,500 jumps who knew exactly what to do.

He walked me through specific instructions prior to our take-off, but nothing prepared me for the rush now coursing through my body.

I realized my life was completely in the hands of this man, so I did everything he told me to do. As I began to take in the sprawling view around me, our descent became graceful, peaceful.

4,000 feet from our landing site, the instructor skillfully maneuvered our position and yanked the ripcord at precisely the right time. Bullseye! We landed in the dead center of our target.

If I had not surrendered my fears during the tandem jump, I would have missed the full experience. It reminds me the most exciting moments as a follower of Jesus occur when I fully surrender my life in the hands of Jesus.

## What Does It Mean to Surrender?

Surrender is giving complete control of your life to Jesus, which can be more complex than it sounds. The act of surrender can generate stubborn emotions of intimidation, fear, and doubt. What if God asks you to move to Africa to be a missionary? What if he wants you to join a convent, become the pastor of a church, or give up friends, relationships, or habits? Questions like those may prompt you to cry out, "Oh, Lord, I believe; help my unbelief!" (Mark 9:24).

In many cases, we are so accustomed to our life that we are unwilling to surrender. I get it. The thought of giving up our lifestyle or possessions is too difficult. We've worked hard for what we have. But the life God has in store for us when we surrender to him is far more satisfying and fulfilling than any material wealth or worldly plans imaginable.

## Roadblock to Surrender: FEAR

Fear is a weapon the Enemy uses to cause doubt when we take steps toward the life Jesus has for us. The root of anxiety is fear, excessive anxiety leads to depression, and deepened depression exacerbates fear—a killer cycle the Enemy uses to distract and defeat us. Think of the word *fear* in terms of the following acronym: **F**alse **E**vidence **A**ppearing **R**eal.

The fear of change often contributes to the unwillingness to surrender. Even people in adverse living situations—abusive relationships, poor living conditions, or grueling and unrewarding occupations—find it hard to choose change. It may seem exhausting, overwhelming, even impossible. Leaving or changing such difficult situations would provide logical benefit. But instead we choose a false sense of security found by filling heart voids with the adversity rather than risking a step forward in faith.

Fear of failure, rejection, and the unknown can also prevent us from surrendering to Jesus. These feelings may have started when we were young, receiving criticism or rejection from parents, peers or coaches. Each time we poured ourselves into a relationship, sport or hobby, the Enemy was right there, reminding us of our failures.

Some of us may even fear success, which stems from our human tendency to be concerned about the growing expectations of others when we are successful. Fear forces us to settle for mediocrity.

Failure in our walk with Jesus only happens when we do nothing—not when we make mistakes!

God uses mistakes as teaching moments to mature our faith. Doing nothing results in missed opportunities to witness the power of God move in our life. In all my years of walking with Jesus, he has not asked me to do anything that he had not prepared my heart to take on with joy. When we faithfully seek Jesus, he helps us live out our life's purpose with great passion: "Delight yourself in the LORD, and he will give you the desires of your heart" (Psalm 37:4).

Surrendering in your walk with Jesus allows you to free-fall into his guidance. Start with the initial steps the Holy Spirit prompts you to take. When you do, you will no longer focus on the worry that held you captive to fear. Instead, the focus is your freedom to walk forward as a fearless child of God.

## Roadblock to Surrender: Human Perception

A builder uses a plumb line to ensure walls are constructed vertically accurate. The builder knows, if his constructed wall follows the plumb line, the wall will be straight and true to the design. This ensures the accuracy of his work.

God provides an instrument of accuracy, the Bible, as our spiritual plumb line to measure the inaccuracies, or fallacies, of human perceptions:

> "This is what he showed me: behold, the LORD was standing beside a wall built with a plumb line, with a plumb line in his hand. And the LORD said to me, 'Amos, what do you see?' And I said, 'A plumb line'" (Amos 7:7–8).

What are some common fallacies of human perception?

1.  I am in control of my life and my destiny.

> "Many are the plans in the mind of a man, but it is the purpose of the LORD that will stand" (Proverbs 19:21).

Thinking you are in control is a fallacy. In my tandem-jump experience, my instructor and I started our descent in an awkward position, causing us to flip-flop from side to side, instead of falling freely. He kept kicking at my right leg because I was attempting to control the position of my leg. Once I relaxed and submitted to the expertise of my instructor, he stabilized our motion and brought us both into the correct free-falling position. Our momentary chaos transitioned to peace when I submitted to his lead.

The same principle holds true in your walk with Jesus. Release control and allow God to take over your circumstances. He will dispel the chaos and instill peace. Sometimes a swift "kick" from God will motivate you to surrender whatever is preventing you from walking in freedom. Surrender does not mean you sit around and wait for God to do all the work. Do your part. Pursue with diligence and discipline what God has already revealed to you.

2. I know what will happen next and what tomorrow will bring.

> "Come now, you who say, 'Today or tomorrow we
> will go into such-and-such a town and spend a year
> there and trade and make a profit'—yet you do not
> know what tomorrow will bring. What is your life? For
> you are a mist that appears for a little time and then
> vanishes" (James 4:13–14).

How often do plans work out as you predicted? How often are you able to determine, in advance, what others will do or say? Your comprehension of this world and your life is finite. Only God's wisdom is infinite and all knowing.

3. I know what is best for me.

> "For my thoughts are not your thoughts, neither are
> your ways my ways, declares the Lord. For as the
> heavens are higher than the earth, so are my ways higher
> than your ways and my thoughts than your thoughts"
> (Isaiah 55:8–9).

God knows what is best for you because he has both a heavenly and an eternal perspective. God gives you freedom to do as you will, but if you turn to Jesus and live according to his wisdom, you will never be led astray. You can then walk in the center of God's will.

When you take your eyes off yourself and fix them on the One whose knowledge and love are infinite, you will discover the truth of God's promises. The opposite of a fallacy is biblical truth, God's plumb line.

## God's Promises about Surrender

To motivate us to surrender, without fear, God gave us many promises. They provide the proper perspective on surrender.

1. God is in control, not me.

> "I am the Alpha and the Omega," says the Lord God,
> "who is and who was and who is to come, the Almighty" (Revelation 1:8).

God is the *Alpha*, beginning, and the *Omega*, end. He has been in control forever, before he created the world, and he knows how everything will end.

2. I am a child of God.

> "For all who are led by the Spirit of God are sons of God. For you did not receive the spirit of slavery to fall back into fear, but you have received the Spirit of adoption as sons, by whom we cry, 'Abba! Father!' The Spirit himself bears witness with our spirit that we are children of God" (Romans 8:14–16).

Identity as a child of God is not determined by race, gender, physical attributes, or profession (John 1:12). These characteristics may be determined by birthplace and where or how you live, but they do not influence identity as God's child. When you believed in Jesus as Lord and Savior, he adopted you into his family.

> "I praise you [God], for I am fearfully and wonderfully made. Wonderful are your works; my soul knows it very well" (Psalm 139:14).

God created each person as a unique individual. Your DNA is different from anyone else's on the planet. You did not "just happen." No one is a mistake.

3. I am an heir to God's kingdom.

> "And if children, then heirs—heirs of God and fellow heirs with Christ, provided we suffer with him in order that we may also be glorified with him" (Romans 8:17).

An *heir* is someone legally entitled to take ownership of another's property upon death. Belief in Jesus' death and sacrifice qualifies you as an heir. As his child you have access to God, his kingdom, and the promises in the Bible. Most importantly, he longs for you, his heir, to understand he is all you need.

4. If I ask according to God's will, I will receive.

> "Ask, and it will be given to you; seek, and you will find; knock, and it will be opened to you. For everyone who

asks receives, and the one who seeks finds, and to the
one who knocks it will be opened. Or which one of you,
if his son asks him for bread, will give him a stone?"
(Matthew 7:7–9).

This text does not imply carte blanche. You cannot ask for whatever
you want and expect to receive it. Instead, seek God's will—knock
on his door and ask his advice through prayer. He will provide what
he knows you need in each situation.

5.  As I surrender to Jesus and serve him, he will reveal his plans
    to me.

"For I know the plans I have for you," declares the
Lord, "plans for welfare and not for evil, to give you
a future and a hope. Then you will call upon me and
come and pray to me, and I will hear you. You will seek
me and find me, when you seek me with all your heart"
(Jeremiah 29:11–13).

Serving God is not just acts of service. It includes seeking his desire
for your life, as well as serving others in the way he directs. God
reveals his plans when you fully surrender to serving him.

## Is There a Biblical Example of Surrender?

Isaiah, a prophet in the Old Testament, had an unshakable faith
and trust in God. In Isaiah chapter 6, God convicted Isaiah to get
his heart right with God. In the presence of God, Isaiah exclaimed,

"Woe is me! For I am lost; for I am a man of unclean lips" (6:8). He confessed his sins and realized the disparity between his humanness and God's holiness.

In an amazing display of God's grace and mercy, an angelic being flew over to Isaiah and "having in his hand a burning coal that he had taken with tongs from the altar. And he touched my [Isaiah's] mouth and said: 'Behold, this has touched your lips; your guilt is taken away, and your sin atoned for'" (Isaiah 6:6–7).

Like all of us Isaiah was sinful, yet God did not condemn him. God forgave Isaiah, cleansing and removing his guilt. This illustrates how God looks at the heart, not the sin. God sees what he created us to be; he does not focus on the person who has made poor choices.

By God's grace, Isaiah transformed from *a man of unclean lips* to an inspired, empowered servant who accepted the challenge God then presented. Speaking on behalf of himself [Jesus, the Holy Spirit, and the heavenly host of angels] in Isaiah 6:8b, God says, "Whom shall I send, and who will go for us?" He was not specifically requesting that Isaiah go, but expressing the opportunity to share a message with the Jewish nation. Isaiah had the freedom to choose and responded, "Here I am! Send me!"

How can you apply Isaiah's situation to your life? He did not ask God for details about what he was to do, nor did he place stipulations on God's call to be a prophet who would speak piercing words about sin and repentance to the people of Israel. Instead, in the presence of God, Isaiah comprehended the eternal importance of the request and said, "I am all in!" That is what surrender to Jesus looks like. Say yes to God and all he has prepared for you. Say, "Here I am! Send me!"

Some Christians consume their existence with past failures and believe God cannot use them. That kind of thinking is a lie, perpetrated by other people and by the Enemy. Release the past and live in the glory and forgiveness of God. The Bible cites stories of people who received second chances and you deserve one as well. Stand strong in the knowledge that God is for you.

## How Do You Know If You Are Fully Surrendered?

Only a few Christians completely surrender to Jesus. Why? Maybe they misunderstand what it requires. The term *surrender* does not imply a careless leap into things we think God wants us to do. It refers to taking faith steps to live in God's will by surrendering ours.

Prior to jumping from the aircraft, my tandem partner coached me through everything necessary to safely jump from the plane. We did not slide into our gear and leap into thin air without first preparing our minds and bodies for the dangerous feat. Isaiah did not randomly jump in to share God's message with the people of Israel. God prepared Isaiah's heart to accept the calling as a prophet. A *call* is a mission or life purpose God has prepared us to live out with an underlying eternal vision.

Prepare your heart to live completely for Jesus. Lay aside your will and expectations. Choose God's will instead. God is preparing you now to know him intimately. He is teaching you how to stand strong against the Enemy and equipping you for his purpose. Through this intentional preparation, you will recognize God's call and be prepared to surrender to him by saying, "Here I am! Send me."

## Take Action

**1.** What are you holding on to that is more important to you than Jesus? Are you willing to surrender it to him?

**2.** What triggers fear in your soul? Journal the Enemy's tactics you recognize in your faith walk with Jesus.

## Next Step on the Path

What does it mean to take up your cross and follow Jesus as he calls us to do in Luke 9:23–25? Read those verses to prepare for the next chapter.

*Chapter Fifteen*

# What Does It Mean to Take Up My Cross?

Jesus chose to pay the price of our sin so we may choose to give him the weight of our cross.

As parents of two school-aged children, Lory and I watch our kids load their backpacks, computer bags, and lunchboxes for school each morning. The amount of baggage they carry to and from school each day astounds me. Because he runs track, our son takes an additional backpack, which he wears on the front of his body, to carry his running shoes, uniform, and water bottle. Why do our schools require students to carry such heavy loads every day? The excess weight affects their posture and can injure their spines.

Many Christians believe Jesus was referring to a similar heavy load in this Scripture:

"And he [Jesus] said to all, 'If anyone would come after me, let him deny himself and take up his cross daily and follow me. For whoever would save his life will lose it, but whoever loses his life for my sake will save it. For what does it profit a man if he gains the whole world and loses or forfeits himself?'" (Luke 9:23–25).

When we read *take up his cross daily*, we may think of Jesus carrying a heavy wooden beam up the hill on the day of his crucifixion. To bear a similar weight seems too difficult. Besides, what loving Father would ask his children to carry such a burden? And why would any God-loving person choose to do it?

## What Does "Take Up [Your] Cross" Mean?

In chapter 5 we discussed the power of what happened at the cross. Now we must understand and believe the significance of the cross if we expect abundant life with Jesus Christ. Let's study Jesus' command line by line:

*If anyone would come after me, let him deny himself.* Jesus does not force us to choose him. He invites. If we accept the invitation to follow him with our actions and beliefs, we must be all in, with no stipulations attached to what God may request. No conditions or only-ifs, one foot in, one foot out. Following Jesus requires our faithful belief we are making the right decision.

Choosing Jesus takes an additional step—denial of self. To *deny* ourself is to say 'no' to finding satisfaction in the what the world offers. And 'yes' to live for the purpose Jesus has for us.

*Take up his cross daily and follow me.* This phrase does not mean Jesus wants us to carry a physical wooden cross. Nor is Jesus implying we fill our life with nothing but baggage to haul around, like my children with their backpacks.

The primitive Greek form of the word *take* means to lift or raise up. Jesus wants us to hand off our burdens to him. He knows the earthly hardships weighing us down and keeping our soul staked to the ground, like the elephant calf in chapter 9. Because Jesus was fully God and fully human, he knows he is the only one who can remove those stakes. Jesus chose to pay the price of our sin, a cost we cannot bear, so we may choose to give him the weight of our cross.

"For to this you have been called, because Christ also suffered for you, leaving you an example, so that you might follow in his steps" (1 Peter 2:21).

Taking up our cross daily is a perpetual expression of looking to Jesus. God allows us to encounter burdens—temptation, suffering, frustration, anger, jealousy, pain, grief—so he can use these situations to refine our soul. He doesn't ask us to focus on the physical burdens but on the spiritual joy experienced when we surrender those struggles at the cross (see chapter 5).

*For whoever would save his life will lose it, but whoever loses his life for my [Jesus'] sake will save it* (emphasis mine). If I desire to have eternal life, I will lose my life through salvation and surrender to him. A surrendered follower of Jesus no longer lives for himself. As a kingdom focus replaces the "me" mentality, our actions glorify God. As the Holy Spirit communes with our spirit, we respond to Jesus' call to put others before ourselves.

*For what does it profit a man if he gains the whole world and loses or forfeits himself?* This portion of the passage refers to the wide path of destruction many take. In the study of Solomon's life in chapter 2, everything under the sun became meaningless as he pursued all the world offered. Jesus warns if we travel the wide path as Solomon did, our life will be meaningless. But surrendering to Jesus gives us everything we need in him.

## How Do You Take Up Your Cross?

What dies at the cross of Christ resurrects to the fullness of life when we completely surrender to Jesus. Over the past twenty years, Jesus has freed me from hooks set deep in my heart—some I knew nothing of until the Spirit revealed them to me. In the book of Ephesians, the apostle Paul explains how to surrender everything at the cross:

"To put off your old self, which belongs to your former manner of life and is corrupt through deceitful desires, and to be renewed in the spirit of your minds, and to put on the new self, created after the likeness of God in true righteousness and holiness" (Ephesians 4:22–24).

## Put Off Your Old Self

To *put off your old self* means self-denial: replace ourselves as the center of our existence with Jesus and his will for our lives. We battle sin, strongholds, and soul ties from which only Jesus can free us (see chapter 9). A soul tie is an unhealthy spiritual connection between two people. Our part in dying to self and sin is to make the firm decision to intentionally choose Jesus, asking him to release us from the stakes of sin pinning us to the ground and transform us by following these steps:

## Step 1: Repent

Recognize sin and turn toward Jesus. Resist your sin by *repenting*, a figurative and spiritual gesture of surrendering your sins to Jesus at the cross. Believe he will deliver you.

[Jesus said,] "The time is fulfilled, and the kingdom of
God is at hand; repent and believe in the gospel"
(Mark 1:15).

## Step 2: Renounce

Ask Jesus to forgive you. To cleanse you of generational soul ties, unhealthy relationships, and strongholds. Ask him to break all curses against you and to demolish Satan's charges contradicting who you are in Christ. I recommend writing names and circumstances, then confess them to Jesus with intentional resolve to avoid them in the future.

"If we confess our sins, he is faithful and just to forgive
us our sins and to cleanse us from all unrighteousness"
(1 John 1:9).

## Step 3: Forgive

Forgive others who have wronged and hurt you as the Holy Spirit unveils names or faces in your mind. Only the Spirit knows the people you have not forgiven. Some of the names he reveals may surprise you. One by one, call out these names to Jesus and talk to him about your feelings.

Jesus may lead you to ask forgiveness from those you offended. This may include a meeting or phone call to correct a wrong and offer contrition. You could also write a letter to someone, even if the person is no longer living. Express your remorse and then either save the letter in a special place or destroy it as an act of ending the bondage of unforgiveness. Jesus will show you what to do.

The good news about forgiveness is it only takes one to forgive. You don't need the other person's permission to offer repentance or forgiveness. Jesus can free you in any circumstance. The other person's response only affects them. Unforgiveness affects you.

Guard your heart and be faithful to follow through with the steps Jesus gives you, no matter how difficult they seem. Jesus knows you are offering or asking for forgiveness to be set free rather than to gain a specific reaction from the other person.

> [Jesus said,] "And whenever you stand praying, forgive,
> if you have anything against anyone, so that your Father
> also who is in heaven may forgive you your trespasses"
> (Mark 11:25).

## Step 4: Stand Firm

Ask Jesus to place the cross between you and the sin, stronghold, or soul tie holding you in bondage and release your spirit and soul.

> "I have been crucified with Christ. It is no longer I who
> live, but Christ who lives in me. And the life I now live
> in the flesh I live by faith in the Son of God, who loved
> me and gave himself for me" (Galatians 2:20).

## Step 5: Receive

Embrace Jesus' forgiveness as he releases you. Then forgive yourself—a critical step. Ask him to fill your heart voids immediately, specific to the sin from which he released you. For example, if Jesus released you from a stronghold of pride, pray he will fill you with his Spirit of humility. If you experience lust, ask Jesus to fill you with his Spirit of self-control. Use a Bible concordance to search for verses relevant to the virtue opposing the sin. Read the verses aloud, repeating them.

> "But the fruit of the Spirit is love, joy, peace, patience, kindness, goodness, faithfulness, gentleness, self-control; against such things there is no law. And those who belong to Christ Jesus have crucified the flesh with its passions and desires. If we live by the Spirit, let us also keep in step with the Spirit" (Galatians 5:22–25).

Other examples of sins and strongholds with their opposing virtue:

> ➤ Hatred or racism: the Spirit of love
> ➤ Discontentment: the Spirit of joy
> ➤ Anxiety: the Spirit of peace
> ➤ Chaotic lifestyle and an overwhelming schedule: the Spirit of order and balance
> ➤ Manipulation and controlling others: the Spirit of kindness and generosity
> ➤ Doubt and fear: the Spirit of confidence and trust

## Step 6: Believe You Are an Overcomer

Believe Jesus has removed the sin and its hooks. Say to Jesus: "I am more than an overcomer through the blood of Jesus and through his forgiveness of my sins."

> "And they overcame him [Satan] by the blood of the Lamb and by the word of their testimony" (Revelation 12:11 NKJV).

## Step 7: Confirm and Seal

Ask Jesus to spiritually cover you with his blood. Pray for Jesus to protect you from the Enemy's sinful hooks returning.

> "But if we walk in the light, as he is in the light, we have
> fellowship with one another, and the blood of Jesus his
> Son cleanses us from all sin" (1 John 1:7).

## Be Renewed in the Spirit of Your Mind

Romans 12:2 instructs us to reject the patterns of this world. Transformation occurs through the renewing of our mind. Godly mental transformation and prayer change our worldview. They lift our eyes from a worldly focus on self to an eternal focus on living for God. Renewal takes place when our minds are released from the bondage of shame, doubt, and guilt of our old self and former manner of life.

## Put on the New Self

To *put on the new self* is to understand and embrace your identity in Jesus. Accept the truth God created you in his own likeness. "So God created man in his own image, in the image of God he created him; male and female he created them" (Genesis 1:27).

We *put on* by believing we are a child of God, an overcomer whose spirit and soul will return to God when we die. When God says to *put on the new self*, he is saying the righteousness and holiness of Jesus are the new clothes we should wear. Clothes cleansed of sin through salvation and sanctification. Adorned with the blood Jesus shed on the cross. A wardrobe completed through his divine resurrection.

Just as Lory and I encourage our children to lighten their backpack load to relieve the physical pressure, Jesus encourages us to unload the heavy, useless layers of our heart—guilt, shame, pain, misunderstanding, doubt, and fear. This spiritual surgery, or sanctification

process, will continue to reveal the nucleus of who we are in Christ—
our new self—as we deny the old self and take up our cross daily.

## Action Steps

**1.** List the burdens you carry around daily. Be specific.

**2.** "Unload your backpack" by following the seven steps outlined
in this chapter and surrendering all the extra weight to Jesus.

## Next Step On the Path

Why is talking to God so vitally important in the life of a follower? Read Matthew 6:5–15 to prepare for the next chapter.

*Chapter Sixteen*

# Why Should I Pray?

Prayer resets life's chaos by bringing us into
the presence of God.

I sat alone on a desolate beach. For hours I prayed and worshiped God—just me and him.

I scanned my surroundings. The full moon shone on a spectacular setting of cool sand under my feet. The crisp ocean breeze wove with my prayers of confession and repentance. His conviction was heavy on me, and I knew I had to first get my heart right with him. I sang praises and danced on the sand. As I wiped the sweat from my brow, I climbed up a lifeguard stand to rest. Not another person in sight. I posed a question to God. Perhaps I hoped for a miracle. "Father, can I walk on water?" Then I added, "No one will see me—it will just be you and me."

Although I did not hear a booming voice come from the sky—as the Bible records in the Old Testament—God's voice bellowed emphatically from within me, "No!" I am not sure what stunned me more—that God answered me so clearly and quickly or that he was so forceful. God continued to impress his word into my heart—not about my impromptu request to walk on water, but about the deeper desire of my heart to serve him.

God's voice—more felt than heard—was a form of conversation. Prayer. Like a two-way discussion. The Spirit trained me to lean in and listen as I sat in the lifeguard stand.

## What Is Prayer?

Prayer is listening and talking to God. Our communication with God helps us recognize the truth in our circumstances. We also learn to see God's amazing blessings by seeking guidance through challenging times. Consider what the apostle Paul wrote to young Pastor Timothy.

> "For everything created by God is good, and nothing is
> to be rejected if it is received with thanksgiving, for it is
> made holy by the word of God and prayer"
> (1 Timothy 4:4–5).

Prayer brings us into the presence of the Father, not to obtain anything from him but to be transformed by him. The truest form of prayer properly aligns our heart as a child of God, with his heart, as our Father. It draws us close to him. But it can also bring conviction of thought or deed as we spend time with him.

Let's look at some fundamentals of prayer.

Prayer is not ...

> ➤ a legalistic act or ritual of the Christian faith.
> ➤ an attempt to use God as a "vending machine."

➤ a performance to show what a biblical scholar we are.

➤ a resort to get ourselves out of trouble.

Prayer is ...

➤ worshiping God, approaching him in humility and reverence (Luke 2:37).

➤ praising God and thanking him for his many blessings (Daniel 6:10).

➤ declaring God's omnipotence (unlimited power) over our requests, concerns, and challenges (Revelation 1:8).

➤ talking with God, privately or in a group, equally expressing ourselves then listening. A good guideline is listening to God twice as much as we speak (Psalm 27:14), highlighting the ratio of ears to mouth.

➤ talking to God about everything and everyone he brings to mind (1 Timothy 2:1).

My night on the beach started with talking to God. With my fingertips, I sketched in the sand the struggles I needed to surrender and the dreams I hoped he would fulfill. God heard me. He set into motion the steps of faith I must take to follow his calling on my life. The Bible says, "The Lord is near to all who call on him, to all who call on him in truth" (Psalm 145:18). I called and God answered.

**Why Is Talking to God Vital?**

The inspiration for my question to God that night on the beach stemmed from Matthew 14:22–33—the story of Jesus walking on water. Following the miracle of Jesus feeding more than five thousand people with five loaves of bread and two fish, Jesus instructed the twelve disciples to board a small boat to cross the Sea of Galilee. Jesus did not go with them. Instead, he chose to spend solitary time in prayer with his Father. When the boat was far from land, storms developed. The waves and a strong headwind battered the hull. Perhaps when Jesus heard the disciples' cries, he decided to walk to the boat through the storm. They were terrified when they saw him approaching, believing he was a ghost. Calmly, Jesus told them, "Take heart; it is I. Do not be afraid" (Matthew 14:27b).

Peter, the most tenacious of the disciples, spoke out, "Lord, if it is you, command me to come to you on the water." Jesus responded, "Come" (Matthew 14:28–29). With the faith and anticipation of a child, Peter climbed out of the boat and walked on the water toward Jesus. Then Peter encountered a test of faith. He became aware of the wind and waves—natural elements causing him to think about the impossibility of what he was doing. Peter began to sink and fearfully cried out, "Lord, save me" (v. 30). In desperation, Peter turned to Jesus and begged for help. He did not use eloquent religious words. Peter responded out of fear in the thick of his storm.

"Jesus immediately reached out his hand and took hold of him [Peter], saying to him, 'O you of little faith, why did you doubt?'" (Matthew 14:31). Although Jesus' action to save his friend was immediate, his statement to Peter caused me to struggle. Jesus seemed to rebuke Peter for faltering in his faith.

Then I saw an artist's rendering of this story. In it, Jesus was smiling, as if to say, "Don't doubt, Peter, I am right here for you, and I love you." Instead of Jesus pointing his finger at Peter with a stern rebuke, the artist's image reminds us of the hope that Jesus instills in us when we trust and believe in him. He pours out his grace and mercy on us when we turn to him.

Jesus answered Peter's prayer quickly. However, we don't always receive an immediate, discernable response from God. This delay may puzzle us because Jesus said, "And whatever you ask in prayer, you will receive, if you have faith" (Matthew 21:22). But the interval may be a test. Why? Waiting and believing that God hears our prayers and will respond, according to his will and his timing, strengthens our faith and trust.

After Jesus and Peter climbed into the boat, the winds stopped. The other disciples looked on in amazement and exclaimed, "Truly you are the Son of God" (Matthew 14:33b). Sometimes we must witness the impossible to know who Jesus really is. Yet this miracle would not have occurred if Peter had not stepped out of the boat. One of twelve disciples took a step of faith and experienced a miracle, while the others looked on. We must climb out of the boat, our comfort zone, and take risks. Stepping out may be the only way to experience the abundance of Jesus—to witness our capabilities through the power of Jesus and prayer.

Prayer is vital because it shifts our focus from self to Jesus. Prayer opens our heart and mind to miracles and aligns our spirit with God's Spirit. Only through prayer can we relinquish control and surrender our circumstances to Jesus, depending on him for the outcome.

Follow these steps:

➤ Listen for God's voice.
➤ Talk to him.
➤ Listen again for his response, or inner promptings, and respond to him in faith.

## What Hinders Prayer?

Have you ever prayed to Jesus but felt as though you weren't connecting with him? Did you become discouraged and lose the desire to pray?

I have learned two broad categories of emotions hinder prayer. Unforgiveness and judgment. Although it seems there are more, when you dig into negative feelings kinking up your prayers, you discover they are rooted in these two emotions. Lory questioned this statement when she first read it. "But what about lust, gossip, gluttony? Those sins hinder prayer." I shared with her all those emotions still boil down to unforgiveness or judgement, which are rooted in pride. Let's look at lust and gluttony, selfishly desiring an object or person we believe we deserve and want to have now. We are judging ourselves because we think we deserve it and judging others because they have it. A spirit of unforgiveness ushers in guilt, depression, anger, and hate. A spirit of judgment produces feelings of unworthiness, shame, belittling, and humiliation. In the story of Jonah, we witness the prophet pouting from feelings of unforgiveness and judgement. He judges the actions of the people of Nineveh and he refuses to forgive them as God has patiently forgiven him.

Holding onto unforgiveness and judgment dams up the spiritual flow of praise and intercession (praying for others). They block our connection to the Holy Spirit, isolating us from Jesus and prevent responses to our prayers. Jesus gave this caution, "And whenever you stand praying, forgive, if you have anything against anyone, so that your Father also who is in heaven may forgive you your trespasses" (Mark 11:25).

## How does unforgiveness hinder prayer?

We live in a fallen world and hurting people hurt other people. When we do not forgive others for hurting us, we permit an unhealthy spiritual stronghold to develop. The stronghold attaches us to the person we hold in contempt. Whether the person is physically present or we continue to relive the act(s) causing pain, their actions still control us. As we relive past hurts, the unhealthy connection controls our mind and negatively affects our clarity and prayers until we surrender our unforgiveness to Jesus.

Forgiving someone does not mean forgetting, excusing, or accepting what he or she has done. Forgiveness releases the person and the pain. The Enemy attempts to entangle unforgiveness in our heart because he wants to sever our spiritual connection and hinder our walk with Jesus. Unforgiveness becomes so deeply rooted, it builds a stronghold. Two friends of ours divorced over forty years ago. They have never forgiven each other, even though they share children and grandchildren. We have witnessed the bitter root of unforgiveness cause division and heartbreak. Likely the situation will not ever change, but if they would choose to surrender it to God instead of holding on, the hearts of their family could begin to heal.

Maybe you have not forgiven yourself for a specific act or poor choice, which leads to shame, guilt, or depression. Perhaps you have not forgiven God for an unexpected loss or long-term illness. Regardless of the cause, your unforgiveness results in a temporary separation from God.

Jesus knows that forgiving yourself and others is a prerequisite to freedom from brokenness and pain. Go to Jesus in prayer and allow him to remove the debris. He will lead you to first forgive yourself, which begins to open your heart to forgive and ask for forgiveness from others. Refer to Chapter 15, Step 3 for guidance in forgiveness.

You may have to forgive yourself or another person multiple times, but you must give yourself the grace to walk through this process. Praying for those who hurt you frees your heart from the debris hindering your prayers. As you forgive, God brings healing that sets you free from the bondage of pain.

## How does judgment hinder prayer?

Judging is the act of elevating self above others, convinced we are better, smarter, more attractive, or more religious than someone else. The root of judgment is pride—making us look better by putting others down. The opposite holds true as well: often we judge ourselves from a negative perspective, feeling as if we do not measure up—could never do what others do or have what they have. We may feel undeserving, unlovable, or unworthy.

Jesus gave clear teaching on judgment:

> "Judge not, that you be not judged. For with the judgment you pronounce you will be judged, and with the

measure you use it will be measured to you. Why do you see the speck that is in your brother's eye, but do not notice the log that is in your own eye? Or how can you say to your brother, 'Let me take the speck out of your eye,' when there is the log in your own eye? You hypocrite, first take the log out of your own eye, and then you will see clearly to take the speck out of your brother's eye" (Matthew 7:1–5).

This Scripture is a warning against hypocrisy. The *log* refers to our sin. Deal with it before pointing out the sin of another. Unlike God, we are not omniscient (all knowing). God desires we view the actions of others through the same filters of grace and love he so graciously lavishes on us. In John 8:7, Jesus admonished a mob of people, ready to stone a woman for her adultery, "Let him who is without sin among you be the first to throw a stone at her." Avoid being the one who claims to have moral behaviors and beliefs not mirrored in our actions. The desire to judge and condemn others will decrease once we begin to see the depth of sin in our own life.

Prayer is most effective when our heart is right with God and others. My ability to discern God's voice as I worshipped and talked with him on the beach had to begin with aligning my heart with his. After I surrendered unforgiveness and judgment, a deep sense of peace came over me as I continued to pray. My mind became quiet, preparing me for God's revelation of what I believe to be the purpose for my existence: to teach others how to walk with Jesus.

When we approach God in a simple yet intentional manner and continually seek his will through prayer, confession, and repentance, our heart will be prepared to hear God's direction.

## Action Steps

1. Set aside an intentional quiet time with God. Reflect on the sections, "Prayer is not…" and "Prayer is…" Journal changes you need to make in your prayer time.

2. Ask God what is hindering your prayers? Listen for his response and journal what he says.

## Next Step On the Path

Jesus gives us a model for prayer. Read Matthew 6:9–13 to prepare for the next chapter.

*Chapter Seventeen*

# How Should I Pray?

Jesus provides a simple model for prayer to
align our will with God's will.

**O**uch! I lifted my bare foot and discovered a tiny metal piston accidentally left out of my model airplane project. I tossed it onto the growing pile of parts laying on the table. Picking up my model, I spun the prop and ran my fingers over the wings. In my 10-year-old mind, it looked identical to the perfectly constructed plane pictured on the box. But in my hurry to assemble the model, I hadn't followed the manufacturer's directions. Now I wondered what purpose the parts served and if my plane would ever fly.

How often do we miss the pleasure of fulfillment because we don't follow the instructions? Prayer is no different. When we approach prayer randomly or rushed, we feel disjointed, like clothes that don't fit just right. When we follow our Creator's model for prayer, our conversation with God refreshes us. Our spirit feels connected with God's Spirit. Because Jesus desires we draw close to him through intimate dialogue, he gives us specific instructions to follow in our prayer life.

## Preparing for Assembly

If I had set out all the parts of my model airplane, comparing each piece to the instructions, perhaps my project would have succeeded. We can prepare for our prayer time in the same way.

Start with being still. Breathe deeply. We are ready to listen when we are quiet and allow the hectic pace of our day to subside. Our mind is more prepared to hear his voice. We don't need to force prayer. Allow it to flow naturally, like laughter and conversation with a best friend. Prayer should be joy-filled. And purposeful. How? By praying according to God's will: "Praying at all times in the Spirit, with all prayer and supplication. To that end, keep alert with all perseverance, making supplication for all the saints" (Ephesians 6:18).

*Praying in the Spirit* sounds complex, but it's not. Think of the Holy Spirit as a coach. A good coach doesn't tell us what to do. He shows us. The Holy Spirit comes alongside us to align our will and prayers with God's.

Our prayer time will not always look the same. My prayers usually begin with thanking God and acknowledging his power. I often marvel at his creativity throughout our world. Sometimes my prayer follows a succinct order. Other times, a shout of praise or cry to Jesus for his intervention. I might begin with my mental list of those in need of healing or salvation. Other times I journal prayers, sing a worship song or recite a prayer from scripture or a devotion.

God does not expect us to pray through the same order or list each time. He desires we spend time in conversation with him. When we allow the Spirit to guide our time with God, we find our prayers aligned with his will.

## How Do We Begin Our Prayer?

God engages with us on a deeply personal level. Each person's interaction with him will be unique, beginning with how we start our prayers. Dear God, Jesus, Heavenly Father, Abba, Daddy, Papa. The great news is, these are all correct and may vary with the type of conversation we are having.

When I pray to the Father, it flows from a place of reverence and honor. Talking with Jesus feels more relational because he walked the earth like me and has felt the same way I might be feeling. My prayers with Jesus feel personal, and I praise him and thank him often each day. Most often, I talk to the Holy Spirit when I seek wisdom and discernment in a situation. Sometimes I talk to all three persons of the Trinity—God the Father, Jesus, and the Holy Spirit—in the same conversation.

Your prayers will differ from mine. You may feel more comfortable talking to Jesus than to God the Father or to God the Father than to the Holy Spirit. What's important is your conversations with each of them mature. You will begin talking to them like close friends as your prayers become more frequent and intentional.

## A Perfect Model for Prayer

In Matthew 5–7, often called the Sermon on the Mount, Jesus teaches a powerful lesson about prayer. His sermon serves as a guide for all followers of Jesus. Chapter 6, verse 5 begins with these words: "And when you pray." Notice Jesus says *when* not *if,* indicating that prayer should be an integral part of a follower's daily life. Jesus provides these instructions:

> "And when you pray, you must not be like the hypo-
> crites. For they love to stand and pray in the synagogues
> and at the street corners, that they may be seen by oth-

ers. Truly, I say to you, they have received their reward.
But when you pray, go into your room and shut the
door and pray to your Father who is in secret. And your
Father who sees in secret will reward you.

And when you pray, do not heap up empty phrases as
the Gentiles do, for they think that they will be heard
for their many words. Do not be like them, for your
Father knows what you need before you ask him"
(Matthew 6:5–8).

Jesus cautions against using prayer to impress people by using eloquent words and meaningless phrases. I organized a prayer team of friends who joined together, praying God's will and interceding on behalf of others. One member was a new believer. At first, she hesitated to pray out loud. But as she gained confidence, we witnessed this young woman pour out the most earnest, simple prayers, filled with raw emotion.

God desires we pray with others (Matthew 18:20), not to glorify ourselves, but to sincerely put God first in prayer. And leave the results to him. Find private, quiet spaces to pray as Jesus did. I enjoy walking wooded paths, absorbing the natural beauty around me and praising God for his creation. I begin by expressing thoughts to God, then listening for his voice.

Jesus gave us the following pattern for prayer in Matthew 6:9–13.

"Pray then like this:
Our Father in heaven,
hallowed be your name"

Our heavenly Father is *hallowed,* meaning sacred or holy. When we express reverence for his power and omniscience, we are declaring our belief God is bigger than all our problems. All evil must submit to his mighty hand because God is the Creator of heaven and earth. Magnify and exalt God the Father and the Lord Jesus who is in heaven.

"Your kingdom come,
your will be done,
on earth as it is in heaven."

Seek God's kingdom here on earth. Jesus knows heaven is perfect and encourages us to pray God will establish his perfect kingdom here on earth. We can pray God will overcome evil through the work of his followers. Pray Jesus will return to gather his followers and call them home to heaven, as the book of Revelation reveals. Pray for the salvation of all those who do not know Jesus, asking God to draw them to him.

"Give us this day our daily bread"

Thank God for his daily provisions. God is the source of all blessings: family, friends, home, job, food, health, wisdom, and joy. Acknowledge his control of daily needs and blessings.

"And forgive us our debts,
as we also have forgiven our debtors"

Ask God to forgive sins. Jesus refers to sin as *debt*. We can ask God to bring sin to mind and seek his forgiveness for each one. Jesus also wants us to express forgiveness toward those who have sinned against us. Giving and receiving forgiveness results in godly freedom we can only experience through Jesus and the power of the cross.

"And lead us not into temptation,
but deliver us from evil."

Pray for God to guard against our weaknesses, warning and protecting us from the temptations of the Enemy. When we ask God to *deliver* us from evil, we are praying he will rescue and redeem us from the evil of the world. Through the work of the Holy Spirit, God makes us aware of the Enemy's baited hooks. We must do our part to fight against evil, too. For example, if we have a tendency to over-eat, we stay away from buffets. If our weakness is pornography, we can install protective software on our computers and seek an accountability partner. As we draw closer to God, his strength restores our energy to fight.

Engage the Lord's Prayer as a foundation by using this acronym:

**P**raise God. Keep your eyes on him. He has authority and power over all creation (Psalm 18:3, 30:4, 145:3; Romans 15:11).

**R**emember to seek God's will and his kingdom, on earth as it is in heaven (Matthew 5:10, 6:10, 6:33).

**A**sk God for daily provisions. Thank him for his continued blessings (Psalm 106:1; Psalm 109:30; Matthew 5:11).

**Y**earn for forgiveness. Forgive others. Deliberately choose to turn from evil and walk with Jesus through your sanctification (Colossians 3:13; Matthew 5:14–15; 1 Thessalonians 5:23).

## Completing the Model

There is great power in ending our prayer "in the name of Jesus" (Acts 2:38, 3:6, 16:18). Why? Jesus means "Savior." His authority as the only one powerful enough to save man from sin gives believers a victorious stance to stand firm in prayer.

The apostle Paul describes the power and authority of Jesus' name in the book of Philippians, chapter 2. Although Jesus is God, he humbled himself "by becoming obedient to the point of death—even death on a cross" (v. 8). Then Paul writes, "Therefore God has highly exalted him [Jesus] and bestowed on him the name that is above every name, so that at the name of Jesus every knee should bow, in heaven and on earth and under the earth, and every tongue confess that Jesus Christ is Lord, to the glory of God the Father" (vv. 9–11). God the Father blessed the faithfulness of his Son, Jesus, who endured the cross to be victorious over sin and death.

In Jude 1:9b Michael the archangel faced Satan, and he fought with a simple command, "The Lord rebuke you." We can stand and pray against evil by engaging the authority of the Lord's name. By ending our prayers with "in the name of Jesus," we acknowledge he is Lord or *Yahweh*—the almighty sovereign God who is always with us. We declare our dependence on Jesus as Savior and as God.

## Navigating Our Takeoff

I have heard Christians say, "ask and you shall receive," an oversimplification of Matthew 21:22, "And whatever you ask in prayer, you will receive, if you have faith." There are misinterpretations of this verse, especially from those new in their faith. Using the phrase as a mantra can be dangerous if our expectations go unfulfilled or we blame God for unfavorable outcomes.

Lory and I searched for a new homestead for months. We searched for acreage with a home we could use for ministry. But the economy was in a seller's market and land prices soared. God closed one door after another until we realized our pursuit of land was not his will, even though our desire for the home was to serve him. Anticipating we will receive whatever we ask for without aligning our desires with

God's, strains our relationship with him. The Enemy can then poison our mind with doubt and bitterness.

How can we avoid asking for blessings in opposition to God's will? Pray in sincere humility, obedience, and faith according to his will, not ours. And pray the scriptures. Jesus provides an example for us from his time just prior to death on the cross. He expressed to God the anguish he felt in his soul. Jesus ended his prayer by asking his Father to take the *cup* (his death on the cross) from him, "Father, if you are willing, take this cup from me; yet not my will, but yours be done" (Luke 22:42 NIV). A simple statement of humility and faith concluded Jesus' conversation with his Father and brought his soul peace.

Follow Jesus' example. Pray his words. Ask God to align your desires with his. Seek to become less of self and more of Jesus. Your fleshly (worldly) desires will shrink to accommodate the growing spirit within you, like replacing a closet full of old clothes with a fresh new wardrobe. A godly transformation begins changing the content of your prayer.

An excitement ignites as your spirit lines up with the Holy Spirit and your prayers turn to praises. You will experience small victories and glimpses of hope because Jesus intercedes for what he knows is best. The dreams and desires of your heart eventually become less self-centered and more Christ-centered.

Jesus wants to help us keep our prayer simple and centered. Like the airplane project years ago, I still occasionally have leftover parts when I don't follow assembly instructions for a complicated home project. When I follow Jesus' model for prayer, I experience deep peace and fulfilment, as he aligns my steps with his.

## Action Steps

**1.** Using the Lord's Prayer in Matthew 6:9–13 and the acronym P.R.A.Y., engage in a conversation with God.

**2.** Journal thoughts that come to you as you pray and spend intentional time with God.

## Next Step On the Path

Jesus says his followers will know and hear his voice. What a comforting promise! Read 1 Kings 19:11–12 to discover where and how Elijah heard God's voice.

## Chapter Eighteen

# Can I Hear the Voice of Jesus?

Jesus wants to talk with you.

I spent years struggling to hear from Jesus, and my frustration was mounting. I read books, attended seminars, and prayed fervently I would hear his voice—yet nothing, not a peep. Finally, while I was on a mission trip to Zimbabwe, Africa, Jesus helped me understand how to listen for his voice.

After I'd given a personal testimony at a church service, a young African woman approached me. She seemed shy, yet determined to share the word God had put on her heart for me. "Stop your striving!" she said emphatically. Then she added if I learned to approach Jesus simply, he would speak to me in a simple way. As I reflected on her words, I knew God was telling me I was working too hard to hear from him. But what did she mean by "simply?"

The only analogy I could materialize was my connection with my father. As a young boy, my dad hung the moon. Our father-son relationship was straightforward and natural, and I looked to my dad for wisdom in all life matters. It occurred to me, as a follower of Jesus, I must view my conversations with Jesus through the eyes of a child.

I wish I could say I heard every word Jesus shared with me after my encounter with the young woman. But I soon realized the bigger issue I needed to address was why the Creator of our universe wanted to communicate with me at all.

## Why Does Jesus Desire to Speak to You?

To hear the voice of Jesus, first believe he wants to communicate with us. Trustworthy, authentic communication is the foundation of any solid relationship. Our Lord and Savior desires to talk to us for many of the same reasons we interact with our loved ones.

Jesus desires to:

➤ draw us close.

➤ share encouragement and hope.

➤ divert our attention from harmful thoughts.

➤ warn us against evil.

➤ provide direction.

➤ protect us from others.

➤ reveal our calling.

➤ lead us in fellowship with others.

## How Do You Tune Your Spiritual Ear to Hear Jesus?

As I continued to lean into hearing from Jesus, an analogy from my pastor helped me understand how Jesus speaks to each of us differently. Modern technology enables us to press one button or speak one voice command and instantly hear the music we want. But years ago, we manually tuned radios to a specific frequency to receive a station's signal. If the frequency wasn't exact, the listener would hear only static—not music or the clear voices of radio personalities.

Jesus desires to speak to us in clear, concise ways. Because God created each person differently, Jesus communicates with us on a frequency unique to every individual. But until we tune our spiritual ear to our particular frequency with Jesus, we hear only static: Is the thought I had from Jesus or was it mine? Did God orchestrate a particular event or was it coincidental? Is the devotion I read or the sermon I heard meant for me, or am I reading too much into it? Not every thought is from Jesus. Not every idea is of God. We must learn to recognize the difference and take some thoughts captive and others we should send to the trash heap.

At first, you may not recognize Jesus' voice. However, as you learn to distinguish his unique way of communicating with you, you will hear what he says. Think of the first time you speak with someone new on the phone. When the person first calls you, he must identify himself. After ongoing communication, you recognize his voice immediately. Jesus' voice may sound like a sweet whisper or a kind inner voice to some. For others he may speak loud or commanding. Jesus approaches me as he did the Old Testament prophets, deliberate, sometimes stern. He gets to the point with me because he knows that is how I hear best.

Recognizing Jesus' voice inspires steps of faith with him instead of stutter-stepping in doubt or fear. To help you tune your spiritual ear to a clear frequency with Jesus, here are seven proven ways he communicates with his followers.

# 1. The Bible.

God's Word is the primary means through which Jesus speaks his undeniable truth. Turn expectantly to the Bible first, seeking answers to questions and confirmation for what you think Jesus is saying. As God told Joshua:

> "This Book of the Law [first five books of the Bible] shall not depart from your mouth, but you shall meditate on it day and night, so that you may be careful to do according to all that is written in it. For then you will make your way prosperous, and then you will have good success" (Joshua 1:8).

By focusing mind and heart on the Word, the Holy Spirit often, but not always, illuminates scripture pertinent to the situation. If I am struggling to lose weight by making better eating choices, the Enemy jumps on every opportunity to cast doubt. Each time I make a poor choice, the Enemy wreaks havoc on my emotions, making me feel like a failure. Until God leads me to Romans 8:37, "We are more than conquerors through him who loved us." God frees my mind by reminding me I am already a conqueror through Jesus.

Jesus speaks specifically through his Word. Jesus speaks specifically through his Word. Other times, a profound peace which surpasses human understanding fills your heart when the Holy Spirit instills a "knowing" about your circumstances. The Bible is alive and powerful. The practice of turning to the Bible protects against stray thoughts or other people's opinions.

# 2. A Quiet Voice.

Separate yourself from life's hectic schedule and take intentional time to rest in Jesus. Remain still, physically and mentally. He may speak to you in a quiet voice only after you have removed all distractions. Rather than limiting Jesus, prepare your heart to listen, as God taught Elijah:

> "And he [God to Elijah] said, 'Go out and stand on the mount before the LORD' And behold, the LORD passed by, and a great and strong wind tore the mountains and broke in pieces the rocks before the LORD, but the LORD was not in the wind. And after the wind an earthquake, but the LORD was not in the earthquake. And after the earthquake a fire, but the LORD was not in the fire. And after the fire the sound of a low whisper"
> (1 Kings 19:11–12).

A low whisper takes quiet and concentration to hear. Start by taking fifteen minutes before daily routines and demands begin. Try taking this intentional time one day a week in a favorite room or chair. Then increase the number of days to two or three, or one weekend a month. For clarity, journal questions or prayers prior to your time with God.

## 3. Devotionals, Other Writings, and Media.

Jesus may use daily devotionals, books, blog posts, or other forms of media to inspire a "hunch"—thoughts or visions in the form of dreams or images you sense in your spirit or perceive in your mind. Although not typical, the hunches are powerful and can paint a picture of future direction or confirmation.

While Jesus speaks through materials other than the Bible, listen carefully before acting on anything outside of his holy Word. Prayerfully ask God to confirm what you read or heard lines up with his will. Something may sound spiritual or godly, but that does not mean it is from God. Satan is a spiritual being operating in the spiritual realm. Satan can mimic God's voice or quote God's words, but he is certainly not one of God's messengers (Genesis 3:1–5).

## 4. Circumstances.

The word *coincidence* does not exist in Hebrew, the original language of the Old Testament. Because God planned everything, there is no coincidence in his plan. Pay attention to unusual circumstances, as Jesus may use them to get your attention. When something coincidental takes place, ask Jesus to clarify anything he is attempting to reveal. For example, I began finding pennies in odd places, on the ground at the gas station, on the treadmill at the gym. Every penny bears the stamp, "In God We Trust." I asked Jesus if the pennies were a message from him. Through devotions and scripture over the next couple of weeks, Jesus confirmed the pennies were reminders to take deliberate steps and "trust in him."

## 5. Consequences.

Jesus allows situations or results in your life as consequences of actions opposing God's Word. His conviction may feel like a heavy hand or spiritual pressure on your soul. "For day and night your hand was heavy upon me; my strength was dried up as by the heat of summer" (Psalm 32:4).

Jesus will not allow uncorrected and unconfessed sin to continue in your life. Conviction will make it uncomfortable for you spiritually, emotionally, and maybe even physically, until you "come clean" through repentance and forgiveness. Arriving home from an unusually heavy work day, I noticed my daughter had not completed a task I asked her to do the night before. I assumed she ignored my instructions and my anger bubbled to the surface as I scolded her harshly. I allowed my emotions to rise to an unhealthy level without checking with Jesus. A heavy, unsettled feeling came over me, which I recognized as conviction, until I apologized to my daughter in front of Lory.

Jesus does not condemn because "There is therefore now no con-demnation for those who are in Christ Jesus" (Romans 8:1). He does allow consequences to communicate his will and bring about con-viction to change. Once you act on his conviction and do the right thing, turning from (or repenting of) wrongdoing, Jesus is merciful and begins the healing process.

## 6. Other People.

Jesus uses other trusted followers to speak wisdom and direction into your life. They may offer hope and encouragement or rebuke and correction, to guide you back onto the path of righteousness. Proverbs 27:17 reminds us, "Iron sharpens iron, and one man sharpens another." Be grateful for the people who love you enough to sharpen you. But seek confirmation through prayer and the Bible when someone says they have a prophetic word from God or something they sense Jesus put on their heart to share. Allow God's Word to validate the counsel you receive from others whom you trust. As your faith matures, you will more easily discern when others are speaking their opinions or God's truth.

## 7. Creation.

God sculpts mountains and valleys and pours water into mighty oceans. He creates animals of all shapes and colors. The light from his sun and moon shift and dance around us. I see brightly colored rainbows adorning the sky, like God had painted it for me to know I can rest in his promises. When we stop to admire nature, all of God's creation reveals his glory, "The heavens declare the glory of God, and the sky above proclaims his handiwork" (Psalm 19:1).

Noah's story in Genesis demonstrates how God used nature to communicate his will and power, and destroy rampant evil. He sent rain for forty days and forty nights. People and animals perished in a great flood that covered the earth. Only Noah, his family, and a selection of animals remained safe in an ark designed by God and built by Noah (Genesis 7:2–3). Following the devastation and cleansing of the earth, God gave Noah this promise:

> "'I have set my rainbow in the clouds, and it will be
> the sign of the covenant between me and the earth.
> Whenever I bring clouds over the earth and the rainbow
> appears in the clouds, I will remember my covenant be-
> tween me and you and all living creatures of every kind.
> Never again will the waters become a flood to destroy
> all life.'... So God said to Noah, 'This is the sign of the
> covenant I have established between me and all life on
> the earth'" (Genesis 9:13–15, 17 NIV).

Jesus desires for you to see him in everything. Listen to God's creation. Tune into what he is saying. Everything you see in nature reflects him and sings his praises (Psalm 95:2–7).

## Keep Your Heart Open

Learning how to distinguish the voice of Jesus takes time and intentional effort. Keep your heart open to him. You cannot put Jesus in a box and limit the ways and methods he will use to talk to you.

Jesus desires a relationship with you. He loves you so passionately, he sacrificed everything at the cross to save you from sin. He talks with you because he promises guidance and direction. As the Father of all creation, "Christ is all, and is in all" (Colossians 3:11b). Why wouldn't he pursue communicating with you, using every part of his Creation? You are a follower of Jesus and your Shepherd covers you with his love and watchful care:

> "I [Jesus] am the good shepherd. I know my own
> [followers in Jesus] and my own know me, just as the
> Father [God] knows me and I know the Father; and

I lay down my life for the sheep [followers in Jesus]"
(John 10:14–15).

I've stopped striving to hear God's voice since I've learned to approach Jesus simply. Tuning to the right frequency enables me to recognize and respond to my Shepherd's voice. As you spend intentional time with Jesus, tune in your spiritual ear and wait for him to speak in simple ways. His voice will become as recognizable as the voice of a loved one over the phone, across a crowded room, or outside on a star-filled night.

## Action Steps

**1.** Do you struggle to hear Jesus' voice? Are you unsure if your thoughts are yours or Jesus' thoughts? Journal what you believe is blocking your spiritual ear from hearing his voice.

**2.** Over the next week, refer to the section "How Do You Tune Your Spiritual Ear to Hear Jesus?" and focus on one of the seven ways Jesus speaks. Write what you hear and turn to God for confirmation of his message.

## Next Step on the Path

What does it mean to abide in Jesus? To prepare for the next chapter, read John 15:1–5.

## Chapter Nineteen

# How Do I Find My Sweet Spot?

The closer we come to Jesus, the more we love.

When I think about the most intimate relationships of my lifetime, my relationship with my dad stands out. I've shared my deepest thoughts and dreams with others, but the one I desire to spend time with is my dad. He recently celebrated his eighty-sixth birthday, and he has influenced every part of my life.

From sailing to golf to fatherhood to career choices and relationships, my dad showed a level of integrity and accountability to which I have aspired throughout my life. As a devout follower of Jesus, he still teaches a weekly adult Sunday school class in his church, leaving a legacy of other believers in his wake. Since childhood, I have grabbed every minute I could to spend with my dad. I still call him to discuss a situation and receive his advice.

Did we always get along well? Of course not. After all, he is my father and, at certain times in my life, we did not see eye to eye. But my reverence, respect, and deep love for him have not wavered.

The relationship between my father and me mirrors the *abiding* relationship Jesus describes in the book of John:

> "As the Father has loved me, so have I loved you. Abide in my love. If you keep my commandments, you will abide in my love, just as I have kept my Father's commandments and abide in his love. These things I have spoken to you, that my joy may be in you, and that your joy may be full" (John 15:9–11).

To *abide* means to dwell or to remain. *Abiding* in Jesus refers to drawing closer to him, coming to know who you are in Jesus, and understanding his calling or purpose for your life. To abide means to rest with him and in him, depending on him for every need as you journey through this fast-paced life. This kind of intimate relationship offers the peace, joy, and acceptance human beings crave. Yet many people live without Jesus or choose an uncommitted, shallow relationship with him. They trudge through their days in their own strength and will.

How can we be certain that we are abiding in Jesus—experiencing the deepest relationship with him? Jesus wants to engage in an intimate relationship with us, beginning with our response to the gospel, or Good News—eternal salvation is only through him.

## The Parable of the Seeds

To help his audience (and us) understand his messages, Jesus often taught in parables, using simple, everyday examples, much like an adult would explain a complex concept to a young child. A parable in the book of Matthew helps us understand how to develop intimacy with Jesus.

A crowd had gathered along the Sea of Galilee to hear Jesus speak. While the people and his disciples listened intently, he shared the story of a farmer who planted seeds in four types of soil. The seeds represent the gospel message and the different soils characterize the ways people receive it.

Jesus used these four scenarios to highlight the fruit each seed bears:

"And he told them many things in parables, saying: 'A sower went out to sow. And as he sowed, some seeds fell along the path, and the birds came and devoured them. Other seeds fell on rocky ground, where they did not have much soil, and immediately they sprang up, since they had no depth of soil, but when the sun rose they were scorched. And since they had no root, they withered away. Other seeds fell among thorns, and the thorns grew up and choked them. Other seeds fell on good soil and produced grain, some a hundredfold, some sixty, some thirty. He who has ears, let him hear'"
(Matthew 13:3–9).

## The First Handful of Seeds: The Good News Is Rejected

These seeds "fell along the path, and the birds came and devoured them" (Matthew 13:4). In this group, the people hear the gospel message, yet they either do not believe it or do not understand its meaning, so they reject it. They reject the truth because their heart, or soil, is hardened. The birds represent the Enemy, his demons, and the idols of the world, which *devour* the seeds of truth, leaving these people unfazed by what they heard.

Their encounter with truth ends quickly, as they continue on the wide path to destruction. The apostle Paul explained the rejection of the gospel this way: "The god of this age [the Enemy, Satan] has blinded the minds of unbelievers, so that they cannot see the light of the gospel that displays the glory of Christ, who is the image of God" (2 Corinthians 4:4 NIV).

What is the destiny of those who reject the gospel message and do not believe in Jesus as their savior? With vivid imagery, Jesus describes their destiny: "If anyone does not abide in me he is thrown away like a branch and withers; and the branches are gathered, thrown into the fire, and burned" (John 15:6).

Biblical scholars believe Jesus' words foretell the damnation of souls who are sentenced to hell for turning their backs on him. These people refuse the gospel message that Jesus is the prophesied Savior of the world. Hell is real; the Bible describes it as an eternal abyss (Matthew 10:28, 16:18; 2 Peter 2:4).

## The Second Handful of Seeds: The Good News Does Not Grow Deep

The next batch of seeds *fell on rocky ground, where they did not have much soil* (Matthew 13:5). These people hear the gospel and grow quickly, with great joy. Tragically, the soil for these seeds is too shallow; the sun scorches these seeds, and they wither and die. Jesus said this kind of person "has no root in himself [Jesus], but endures for a while" (Matthew 13:21a). The seeds of truth do not penetrate the soul more than surface deep, and therefore the person cannot grow roots. Those who experience Jesus in this way do not let the farmer (God) *cultivate* their heart. The truth lies near the surface of their heart, and when conflict arises, these people fall away and follow the path of least resistance: "Blessed is the one who fears the LORD always, but whoever hardens his heart will fall into calamity" (Proverbs 28:14).

## The Third Handful of Seeds: The Good News Is Choked by Worldliness

These seeds "fell among thorns, and the thorns grew up and choked them" (Matthew 13:7). These people hear the truth, "but the cares of the world and the deceitfulness of riches choke the word, and it proves unfruitful" (v. 22b).

The thorny ground represents those who are consumed by the worldliness of feeding their own desires. Although the gospel truth has penetrated their heart, the world still consumes their soul. They become spiritually paralyzed, with one foot on the wide path and one on the narrow path. Instead of abiding in a relationship with Jesus, they resist change and take control of their lives.

As they experience constant conflict in their soul, they waver between the conviction of truth and the worldly circumstances that lead them to dabble with former sinful behaviors. The *thorns* continue to *choke* these individuals, causing them to miss their eternal purpose *unless* they firmly commit to walk faithfully as a follower of Jesus. In the book of Revelation, Jesus admonished this type of double-minded follower: "I know your works: you are neither cold nor hot. Would that you were either cold or hot! So, because you are lukewarm, and neither hot nor cold, I will spit you out of my mouth" (3:15–16).

## The Fourth Handful of Seeds: The Good News Grows and Thrives

These seeds "fell on good soil and produced grain, some a hundredfold, some sixty, some thirty" (Matthew 13:8). The *good soil* represents pliable hearts ready for cultivation. The message of salvation enriches the lives of the followers, so they allow themselves to be pruned, or sanctified, by Jesus. Their relationship with Jesus is characterized by their "fruit and yields, in one case a hundredfold, in another sixty, and in another thirty" (v. 23).

But pruning sounds painful. What does Jesus need to get rid of so we can abide in him and bear fruit?

## Abiding in Jesus: The Pruning Season

North Carolina weather provides residents with four distinct seasons for planting and pruning. Each spring Lory and I enjoy filling our yard with rose bushes, lantana and other seasonal plants. Throughout summer and fall, we trim the leggy, non-flowering branches which prevent new growth, cutting some plants down to nothing but a stalk. Pruning allows natural nutrients from the soil to nourish new growth in the dormant season and produces a symphony of color each spring.

Jesus provided his listeners with a similar visual of a grapevine pruned by a vinedresser. The audience in his day could easily relate to his example of cutting away unproductive branches until the fruit is dependent on the vine:

> "I [Jesus] am the true vine, and my Father is the vine-dresser. Every branch in me that does not bear fruit he takes away, and every branch that does bear fruit he prunes, that it may bear more fruit. Already you are clean because of the word that I have spoken to you. Abide in me, and I in you. As the branch cannot bear fruit by itself, unless it abides in the vine, neither can you, unless you abide in me. I am the vine; you are the branches. Whoever abides in me and I in him, he it is that bears much fruit, for apart from me you can do nothing" (John 15:1–5).

Jesus refers to himself as the *true vine,* meaning the Messiah sent to save all people from their sins. The *vinedresser* is God the Father, Creator of heaven and earth, who owns the vineyard and oversees its growth. Jesus' listeners, primarily Jews, would have immediately recognized the importance of these words, as the Old Testament referenced the vine and vineyard as a symbol of Israel (See Psalm 80:8; Isaiah 5:1–7; Jeremiah 6:9, 12:10). Jesus explained bearing fruit for God's kingdom requires a spiritual pruning like the grapevine needs pruning to maximize its harvest.

## Spiritual Pruning

What does spiritual pruning involve? When I said yes to an abiding relationship with Jesus, I surrendered my will for his will. My pruning process is now 32 painful, beautiful, liberating years in the making. God's transformation in me is like turning a new pair of jeans inside out. He is more interested in the inner seam of my spirit and soul working together than my outward appearance. For too long I focused on the new-pair-of-jeans life, how it looked and felt. My life was all about my career, income, relationships, and a secure future.

But God turned my love of self inside-out. Where he hacked away selfishness, he grew my desire to seek his will. Where he severed unforgiveness, patience and grace flourished. What felt like spiritual amputation at times made me realize, if the inner stitching of my heart is not right, what I look like on the outside does not matter.

God prunes his vine to remove *every branch ... that does not bear fruit* (15:2). Jesus referenced this in the third group of seeds falling among the thorns. The thorns eventually choked the healthy growth so the seed could not bear fruit.

Are you ready to allow God to cut away? Are you willing to have your pet project pruned? Writers must face the editor and watch their beautiful words marked out. Filmmakers watch as their favorite part of the movie lands on the cutting room floor. Parents watch as dreams for their children fade away and the child's dream blossoms.

But pruning isn't just about cutting away. It's also about the desire for deep personal change: are you willing to prune sin from your heart? If I have unforgiveness in my heart, I cannot serve him in the best way. If I allow ambition to rule in my interactions in church, I will always fall short. If I fail to give generously, God will not bless me generously. If I hold hate in my heart, I won't know the full extent of God's love. When Jesus reveals the sin that opposes his will, he invites you to surrender the sin to him.

This pruning process is sanctification, your lifelong spiritual growth, which can even leave you feeling empty for a while. Jesus will not allow you to depend on anyone or anything (idols) but him. God the Father, the vinedresser, removes the sins and heart voids so you can experience an abundant life with Jesus.

## Abiding in Jesus: Bearing Fruit

Fruit is the tangible impact our life has on others when we live by faith and point people to Jesus. As God removes the debris of sin, the love of Jesus flows through a believer's heart to touch others because we become an extension of his love. This desire to bear much fruit wells up from within, due to the heart transformation taking place. Serving with an expectation of earning God's love, or the love of others, can only end in disappointment. God prompts us to serve and love others, not to earn love but from a place of love. Jesus explained it this way: "By this my Father is glorified, that you bear much fruit and so prove to be my disciples" (John 15:8).

The climatic result of persevering through sanctification is learning why God created us and his plan for us to bear fruit: our spiritual sweet spot. Our sweet spot comes naturally to us because it's our purpose—what he created us to do in this world for him. God reveals and allows us to fulfill our purpose only when we remain faithful to him. Our preparation to fulfill our purpose takes a great deal of time in our walk with Jesus, because God is more concerned with what we become than what we do.

# Abiding in Jesus: Loving Others As Jesus Loves You

A scribe (one who interpreted and recorded information regarding the Jewish Law) once asked Jesus to identify the most important of God's commandments. Jesus answered, "And you shall love the Lord your God with all your heart and with all your soul and with all your mind and with all your strength. The second is this: You shall love your neighbor as yourself. There is no other commandment greater than these" (Mark 12:30-31).

What is the ultimate result of an abiding relationship with Jesus? Love. We learn how to love Jesus, ourselves, and others. Loving Jesus draws us deep into relationship with him. It nurtures a desire to follow his lead. And develops a friendship built on trust, mutual affection, and admiration but always coupled with awe and reverence for his sovereignty and holiness.

Jesus loves us as a friend and unveils himself to us so we can reveal him to others. This love prompts the Holy Spirit to speak to and guide us daily. God so loved the world that he gave from the depths of his heart, his only Son, Jesus, to die for our sins (John 3:16). Jesus chose the cross because he loves us. He expects and equips us to do the same for others, as he loves through us.

Jesus ends the parable of the vine with these words:

"This is my commandment, that you love one another
as I have loved you. Greater love has no one than this,
that someone lay down his life for his friends. You are
my friends if you do what I command you. No longer
do I call you servants, for the servant does not know
what his master is doing; but I have called you friends,
for all that I have heard from my Father I have made
known to you. You did not choose me, but I chose
you and appointed you that you should go and bear
fruit and that your fruit should abide, so that whatever

you ask the Father in my name, he may give it to you.
These things I command you, so that you will love one
another" (John 15:12–17).

Those outside the Christian faith can exhibit love, but only Jesus followers can model true, deep, compassionate Christlike love demonstrated through actions and words. A heart bears fruit when it loves people and isn't choked by the world. Laying down our life for him and for one another—this is love for a world that needs Jesus, now more than ever.

I believe God provides relationships in your life to sustain you through spiritual seasons. Seasons of pain, rejoicing, learning, loving. My relationship with my dad prepared me for the depth of intimacy God wants with me. Your heavenly Father first chose you *and appointed you that you should go and bear fruit* by remaining connected to the vine in an abiding relationship with Jesus.

## Action Steps

**1.** Using the parable of the seeds, identify which set of seeds best describes your spiritual journey.

**2.** What step can you take now to seek a deeper relationship with Jesus? Journal your step.

## Next Step On the Path

Is it really possible to be holy? Read 1 Peter 1:13–16 to prepare for the next chapter.

## Chapter Twenty

# What Does It Mean to Live Holy?

*Holiness is not about what you do. It's about who you become in Jesus.*

When we started dating, Lory and I made the commitment to Jesus that we would remain pure (sexually abstinent) prior to marriage. We had both experienced an array of challenges, heartbreak, and pain in previous marriages. We were determined to court each other according to God's will, knowing that our relationship had been divinely orchestrated. God brought us together for a purpose well beyond our love for each other. We had a fresh start and a clean slate. We wanted to enjoy the romance without falling into lustful passions driving us to the physical side of love prior to our marriage. We took the call to personal holiness in 1 Peter 1:14–16 seriously:

"As obedient children, do not be conformed to the
passions of your former ignorance, but as he who called
you is holy, you also be holy in all your conduct, since it
is written, 'You shall be holy, for I [the Lord] am holy'".

Since the day Lory and I met, our profound love for each other has
affected our hearts, souls, and bodies to desire each other with great
passion. Yet, through a series of scriptures and daily devotions, prayer
and fasting, God continued to remind us he was with us, and he
prompted us to remain holy. Our love was growing and our passion
increasing. Waiting became increasingly more difficult.

Around that time God showed us he meant business. I was driving to
the market to shop for the coming week. Lory and I were struggling
with the whole abstinence subject, and I asked God for strength and
resolve. As I approached a traffic stop, the license plate directly in
front of me caught my attention. It read, BE HOLY. I grabbed my
phone, snapped a picture, and texted it to Lory. God had sent us a
message.

About an hour later, Lory was driving in the opposite direction and
saw the same car and license plate, BE HOLY. She snapped the
picture and sent it to me. As we talked by phone, conviction quickly
subdued our initial amazement. God's love for us was so profound
he would do anything to get our attention. He knew what was best
for us—our future marriage together would allow us to celebrate
physically what God was doing in us spiritually. Again and again,
God reminded us of this scripture:

"Flee from sexual immorality. Every other sin a person
commits is outside the body, but the sexually immoral
person sins against his own body. Or do you not know
that your body is a temple of the Holy Spirit within
you, whom you have from God? You are not your own,

for you were bought with a price. So glorify God in
your body" (1 Corinthians 6:18–20).

Does the fact that we waited make us holy? How is it even possible
to be holy if we are born into sin? Can any of us achieve holiness
through our actions and determination to do the right thing?

## What Is Holiness?

One definition of holiness is "being set apart or dedicated for God's
purpose." But holiness involves more than living by religious principles or church-driven doctrine. It is greater than the dos and don'ts
of social morality.

As we attempt to survive in this world's fishbowl of temptation
and immorality, we will fail. Every follower will succumb to fleshly
pleasures. No one is strong enough to live right, based on actions
(works) or merit. These failures typically leave us feeling miserable
and discouraged, especially when the Enemy repeatedly reminds us
of sinful behavior, which he drapes in guilt and shame.

God created us with human desires and passions. Lory and I knew
God was not trying to prohibit us from expressing our love or
experiencing physical pleasure. We knew what the Bible said about
sexual morality, and we wanted to do the right thing. But as humans
operating in our strength, it was not only sin and temptation that
troubled us but also our self-centered wills. At times, we wanted
to go down the wrong path. If we had allowed our will to create
pockets of sin and darkness in our heart, sin and shame would taint
our marriage. God shouted at us to "Be holy!" because he knew
holiness—in our case, abstinence—would draw us closer to one
another and to him.

As followers, we are set apart, or dedicated, to God's purpose, which
means we belong to Jesus and we are no longer our own (Hebrews
8:10).

## Holiness: Who You Are in Jesus

As you dive deeper into the meaning of holiness, you find God demands more than acts of obedience. Holiness isn't a matter of works—following rules, being religious or a good person, or serving in church. Why? You cannot become holy on your own. Holiness is not what you do—it is who you become in Jesus.

Holy living requires me to realize and understand I am redeemed only by Jesus, united with him because of the price he paid on the cross. The difference between holiness based on living surrendered to Jesus (relationship or inward approach) versus living right through your own strength (works or outward approach) is the redemption of Jesus. As you learn to look at yourself through Jesus' eyes, rather than through your own, you understand his sacrifice on the cross is what clothes you in holiness.

## Holiness: The Salt of the Earth

Since ancient times, salt was used for both preserving and seasoning. As long as the salt remains pure and fresh, it maintains the integrity of the substance it is protecting. Over two thousand years ago, Jesus used the analogy of salt to illustrate righteousness and holiness, warning his followers to remain pure and therefore useful for God's purposes, "You are the salt of the earth, but if salt has lost its taste, how shall its saltiness be restored? It is no longer good for anything except to be thrown out and trampled under people's feet" (Matthew 5:13).

Salt is essential to life and good health. As a follower of Jesus, you are the *salt of the earth,* called to enhance the flavor of life with passion for God's purpose. This analogy of being salt also comes with a warning, however: as you continue your walk with Jesus, your resolve may weaken and you may fall into sin, which compromises your *saltiness* (holiness in Christ). If you allow sin to continue, it will permeate your soul, eventually diminishing or destroying your testimony.

## Holiness: The Light of the World

In the book of John, Jesus describes himself this way: "I am the light of the world. Whoever follows me will not walk in darkness, but will have the light of life" (John 8:12). In Matthew, Jesus refers to his followers in much the same way:

"You are the light of the world. A city set on a hill cannot be hidden. Nor do people light a lamp and put it under a basket, but on a stand, and it gives light to all in the house. In the same way, let your light shine before others, so that they may see your good works and give glory to your Father who is in heaven"
(Matthew 5:14–16).

Jesus calls his followers to shine his light in the world. He desires we live differently, reflecting his attributes like a mirror. This is holy living. When our life reveals more of Jesus and less of self, the image others see is beautifully enhanced by the One who created us. Our journey toward holy living enables us to be image-bearers.

## Baptism: An Outward Expression of Holiness

In the Christian faith, the ceremony of baptism includes sprinkling or immersing an individual in water, symbolizing purification through spiritual conversion in Christ. Jesus gives an example through his own holy baptism: an outward act of inward cleansing.

God requires baptism for all believers in Jesus. Although some religions and church denominations celebrate the baptism of infants and young children, biblical baptism is an act of obedience to God when you profess Jesus as your Lord and Savior. "And Peter said to them, 'Repent and be baptized every one of you in the name of Jesus

Christ for the forgiveness of your sins, and you will receive the gift of the Holy Spirit'" (Acts 2:38).

You can experience salvation in Jesus without baptism, but baptism cannot replace salvation. Only Jesus saves you from sin. Baptism is a part of your testimony following salvation from sin through Jesus' death and resurrection. Mark 16:16b states, "Whoever believes and is baptized will be saved." This public profession of faith emulates Jesus' death on the cross, followed by his burial in a tomb and, finally, his resurrection to life three days later.

Biblical baptism illustrates the death and resurrection of Jesus and the command in Ephesians 4:22–24 to "put off your old self, be renewed in your mind and put on the new self." With the help of someone performing the ceremony, you are immersed backward into the water with your eyes looking toward heaven. This portion of the ceremony symbolizes death with Jesus on the cross: putting *off your old self.*

Remaining momentarily under the water testifies you are dead to self and buried with Jesus. You are choosing to *be renewed in your mind.*

Raising from the water declares your resurrection to life in Jesus, through the power of the Holy Spirit. You put *on the new self* through the same power that raised Jesus from the dead—the power living within you as a follower.

The apostle Paul explains it in Colossians 2:12, "Having been buried with him in baptism, in which you were also raised with him through faith in the powerful working of God, who raised him from the dead." You now have a new life in Jesus, set apart to be holy and glorify him in all you think, say and do.

## Holiness: A Lifelong Pursuit

Is there a point in your spiritual maturity when you can say, "My holiness is complete?" No, your walk toward holiness and sanctification is a continual journey through spiritual maturity on this side of heaven.

But do not become lazy on your journey. Spiritual laziness opens the door to doubt, which leads to spiritual paralysis—an emotional state the Enemy uses to torment you. Many unhappy, unfulfilled Christians (I was one of them!) claim Jesus as Savior, yet they battle and complain about the same struggles year after year. Spiritual laziness is an insult to your faith because God has "given us everything we need for a godly life" (2 Peter 1:3 NIV).

You have God's divine power within you to become holy. Pursue him as if each day is your last day on earth. Human tendency is to believe we cannot be holy. But remember God sees you through the holiness of Jesus. Allow him to shift your perspective to his.

## How Does God Use the Virtue of Holiness in You?

Perseverance toward holiness yields abundant fruit. You will recognize and align your actions with the way God has uniquely shaped you— through the abilities and passions he has put in your heart. When you allow Jesus to move through these godly qualities, you become the *light of the world,* and others will marvel at the works Jesus accomplishes through you.

Lory and I relish all God has done in our relationship. Through our journey toward holiness, he has used us as salt and light to point others to Jesus. Our part is simple: to humble ourselves and be holy as God is holy. God's part ... well, that is the miracle. He has restored two broken people through his power and grace, and engaged us to come alongside others in their suffering, refining, and growth.

God wants to use you as salt and light too. Allow him complete access to your heart. Watch for the miracles he performs in and through you.

## Action Steps

**1.** Describe what holiness can look like in your life. Ask Jesus to confirm this and to give you the opportunity to pursue it.

**2.** Review the four sections beginning with "Holiness." Of the four, which category represents your greatest struggle? Journal the reason why.

## Next Step On the Path

How do you protect your heart and the work Jesus is doing within you? Read Proverbs 4:23 to prepare for the next chapter.

## Chapter Twenty-One

# How Can I Guard My Heart?

Protecting the springs of life guards our
spiritual heart.

Early Christmas morning, I snuck quietly down the stairs of our family home while my parents and sister slept. I was eight years old, and the month leading up to Christmas seemed like an eternity. Would I actually receive the gifts I had been begging my parents to give me? I sifted through the packages, lifting, shaking, and surmising the possibilities within the brightly colored Christmas wrapping.

Later, my sister and I distributed the gifts to each member of the family. It seemed like someone rang an imaginary bell, and we were set free. My sister and I tore into package after package, paper and ribbon flying, leaving a trail of Christmas debris in our wake. Viewing each gift, I felt like my dreams had come true. A fleet of metal Tonka trucks and the accessories to accompany them. I had received the equipment needed for a small construction company.

I marveled at the meticulous detail of each truck and dreamed of how I would use these rigs to dig and move the earth in our sandpit out back. I cleaned my fleet after almost every use. I often slept with my trucks. I lined them up on my bed along one wall, leaving just enough room to slide under the covers beside them. Alongside me, they would be guarded and protected.

I cherish the memories of those Tonka trucks. To a young boy, they were special treasures. But I've learned our earthly treasures grow old and dull, no matter how carefully we protect them. Eventually we lose interest and those objects of affection soon sit on a shelf collecting dust. Matthew 6:19-21 explains:

"Do not lay up for yourselves treasures on earth,
where moth and rust destroy and where thieves break in
and steal, but lay up for yourselves treasures in heaven,
where neither moth nor rust destroys and where thieves
do not break in and steal. For where your treasure is,
there your heart will be also."

Where is your treasure? In what you own or do? The apostle Paul instructs followers to regard your treasure as a *good deposit* or work Jesus is completing within your spiritual heart:

"Follow the pattern of the sound words that you have
heard from me, in the faith and love that are in Christ
Jesus. By the Holy Spirit who dwells within us, guard
the good deposit entrusted to you"
(2 Timothy 1:13–14).

God wants you to guard and protect this gift. But, how?

## Guarding the Work of God

God provides two powerful examples in the Old Testament: the tabernacle and the temple.

The Jewish nation could only worship God in a physical location. God gave Moses detailed instructions for building the tabernacle. God remained present in this place of worship as the Jewish nation traveled through the desert on their way to the Promised Land. Then God revealed the plans for a permanent worship structure—the temple—to King David, who passed them on to his son Solomon (1 Chronicles 28). As in the tabernacle, God resided with his people in the temple. God divinely blueprinted the two structures with three primary sections:

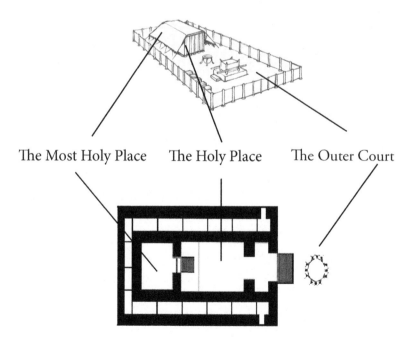

The Most Holy Place    The Holy Place    The Outer Court

**The Outer Court**. The Outer Court was open to the general population, both Israelites and Gentiles. All were welcome to worship there.

**The Holy Place**. The Holy Place was inside the Outer Court. It was concealed from public view and accessible only to priests completing holy rituals to honor God. The books of Exodus and Leviticus describe these rituals in detail.

**The Most Holy Place**. God's Presence and Spirit dwelt in the inner sanctuary called the Most Holy Place. This section was the innermost room of both the tabernacle and temple and was not accessible to the public. The Most Holy Place held the Ark of the Covenant, which contained the stone tablets on which were written the Ten Commandments (Exodus 20). This room was off limits to all people except for the appointed Israelite high priest who could enter once a year, on the Day of Atonement (Hebrews 9:7). The priest offered blood sacrifices for himself and for the sins of the people to atone for their sins and receive God's forgiveness. The priest entered the room through a veil—made of fabric woven from blue, purple, crimson, and white thread, and embroidered with cherubim (2 Chronicles 3:14).

Since God's presence was only in The Most Holy Place, God often spoke to the prophets, giving them divine direction and clear boundaries—and pointing people to the coming of Jesus. In the Old Testament era the Holy Spirit selectively dwelled within an individual for a specific purpose (1 Samuel 16:13). The New Testament changed the landscape for the work of the Spirit. He lives in those who believe in Jesus (John 14:17). A believer's spirit is alive, joined with the Holy Spirit and residing in our spiritual heart.

## Your Temple—Spirit, Soul, Body

God created us in his image. Like the tabernacle and the temple, we are a holy place of worship and must protect the place where God resides, our spiritual heart. Remember, our spiritual heart makes us unique—it's the special part of us which differs from everyone else. Our spiritual heart is filled with the Holy Spirit and requires guarding and protecting. In Proverbs 4:23, King Solomon wrote, "Keep your heart with all vigilance, for from it flow the springs of life." The New International Version helps us understand what Solomon meant. "Above all else, [you should] guard your heart, [because] everything you do flows from it."

Solomon is referring to the deep well (spiritual heart) God digs within every believer. He removes the dirt (sin) and fills the well with free-flowing living water (Holy Spirit). Our spirit commingles with his Spirit in the well.

John 7:38b says "out of his [spiritual] heart will flow rivers of living water." This *water*, symbolic of the Holy Spirit, flows from a never-ending source of pure, uncontaminated spring water, even during the harshest droughts. Our responsibility is to protect the living water with strong boundaries. But how do you guard yourself spiritually and physically and why is it important to God?

In chapter 6, we learned our spiritual heart is comprised of three elements—spirit, soul, and body. To understand the difference between these elements and the importance of protecting them, we'll compare them to the rooms in the tabernacle and the temple.

The Outer Court is like our body. The Holy Place represents our soul. The Most Holy Place reveals our spirit.

## Guarding Your Body, the Outer Court

Your body, the Outer Court, is the part of you exposed to worldly influences and on the front line of spiritual warfare. Think of your body, or flesh, as a reservoir collecting from both the life-giving springs of water within your spiritual heart and your experiences from the outside world. When you choose to guard the Outer Court, you allow others to see the transforming work of Jesus in your life flowing outward, rather than the contamination from the world's unfiltered waters flowing inward. Guarding your body requires these actions:

> ➤ Guard against sin and evil by utilizing God's wisdom in the face of temptation, even if you think you're missing out on something better or more enjoyable (Psalm 86:2).
> ➤ Live humbly, spend and save wisely, minimize debt, and give to the needy (Proverbs 11:25).
> ➤ Honor God by dressing modestly, whether male or female, rather than dressing to attract attention to your body (1 Timothy 2:9).
> ➤ Worship Jesus, lifting your hands to praise him or falling to your knees to pray (Psalm 63:4; Luke 5:8).
> ➤ Endeavor to please the Lord in all your thoughts and actions: how you live, work, and care for yourself spiritually, mentally, emotionally, and physically (Colossians 1:9–10; Psalm 127:2).
> ➤ Respond to others gently and kindly. Hug the hurting. Help the physically and mentally disheartened (Ephesians 4:32).
> ➤ Treat your body with respect and commit to fitness and plenty of rest (Job 33:4).

Others will gravitate toward you as you *guard the good deposit entrusted to you.* They will recognize something is different about you and, often, they want what you have. Of course, you know the difference is Jesus; therefore, remain diligent in setting strong boundaries that keep your reservoir pure.

## Guarding Your Soul, the Holy Place

Your soul is like the Holy Place of the tabernacle, located just inside the Outer Court and accessible only to priests performing rituals. Although the soul is an internal part of every person, you constantly expose your soul to more external stimuli than your body because of receptors: mind, will, and emotions. God enriches the soul with springs of water flowing from the deep well of your heart.

Equating your soul to the Holy Place reveals the importance of protecting the "springs of water." Like the psalmist, we should pray, "Oh, guard my soul, and deliver me! Let me not be put to shame, for I take refuge in you [God]" (Psalm 25:20).

Limit your soul's exposure only to those you trust within your immediate family and to a handful of trusted friends who have proven themselves faithful and godly. Recognize triggers causing spiritual, mental, or physical weakness. Protect yourself from worldly influences leading to destructive actions:

➤ doubting God
➤ relying on the opinions and approval of others
➤ covering up your weaknesses, rather than humbly confessing your sins
➤ allowing yourself to abandon personal boundaries before counting the costs

Trusting others is a delicate subject. God does not want you to be suspicious or callous toward others. He wants you to protect your soul. Protection requires a disciplined eye and an attentive ear to discern red flags from Jesus. You may sense a nudge at your heart or a tug at your thoughts—ways he warns you of someone's negative intentions, including family. Your trust in Jesus will continue to mature, but do not freely expose your soul to others.

Jesus modeled this kind of soul protection during his earthly journey:

> "Now when he [Jesus] was in Jerusalem at the Passover Feast, many believed in his name when they saw the signs that he was doing. But Jesus on his part did not entrust himself to them, because he knew all people and needed no one to bear witness about man, for he himself knew what was in man" (John 2:23–25).

Jesus *did not entrust* himself to others, which means he was cautious of who he allowed close to his spiritual heart. Because Jesus was fully man, he understands how difficult it can be to guard your soul, trusting it only to a few mutually nurturing relationships.

Here are some practical ways to guard the Holy Place:

➤ Give yourself grace when old habits reemerge and cause you to stumble or sin (Ecclesiastes 7:4).

➤ Be cautious confiding the secrets of your soul and the sins that challenge you (Proverbs 27:17).

➤ Hold yourself accountable with a trusted friend who provides wise counsel to help you live within your boundaries. No man, or woman, is an island standing alone spiritually (Proverbs 27:17).

➤ Hold God's revelations about your future work and calling in confidence (Proverbs 20:19).

➤ Avoid taking center stage. Instead, seek to serve others with a joyful heart (Galatians 5:13).

➤ View life's circumstances through the lens of joy and praise rather than negativity, thanking God daily for his many blessings (Psalm 100:4).

➤ Create a bucket list of goals to live an abundant, balanced life (Jeremiah 29:11).

The Spirit helps you in each of these practical actions. The most important step you can take to guard your soul is taking all thoughts captive to Jesus (2 Corinthians 10:5). Jesus is the one you can always trust. And trusting him forms a habit within your soul to guard the springs of living water.

## Guarding Your Spirit—The Most Holy Place

God quickened (gave life) to your spirit the moment you believed in Jesus and prayed for the forgiveness of your sins. The Holy Spirit took up residence in your spiritual heart, which is now your Most Holy Place, or inner sanctuary.

In this divinely intimate spiritual well, the Holy Spirit flows consistently to fill your inner voids—fear, uncertainties, deep wounds—as God reveals their existence. Your faith in him continues to mature when you learn to surrender your will to his, over and over. God's sanctifying work takes place in your spirit, the Most Holy Place.

Within your inner sanctuary you hear God's voice and mature into oneness with him. This connection with God empowers you to emulate Christlike actions flowing through you to others.

Just as the Most Holy Place in both the tabernacle and the temple was off limits to anyone but the high priest and God, the spiritual well should be off limits to everyone, except God and your faithful spouse, with whom you are biblically one in him (Genesis 2:24; Ecclesiastes 4:12).

How can you guard the Most Holy Place where the Holy Spirit resides with your spirit?

➤ Allow God to cultivate the unplowed ground of your spiritual heart as you draw closer to Jesus (Hosea 10:12).

➤ Rest in Jesus. Learn to be still, listening to his voice rather than responding with your thoughts (Psalm 46:10).

➤ Keep a teachable, pliable spirit. Hold on to God's instruction (Proverbs 4:13).

➤ Study God's Word, aspiring to do everything written in it (Joshua 1:8).

➤ Worship Jesus in spirit and truth (John 4:24). Acknowledge Jesus is God and the Holy Spirit lives within you. Establish all you worship in life on the promises and truth of God's Word.

➤ Take up your cross daily to follow Jesus and surrender your will to him (Luke 9:23).

Opening the inner sanctuary only to Jesus and your trustworthy spouse provides freedom. You know you are listening to God's truth and the Holy Spirit is continuing his sanctifying work. Once you experience this abundant life, you will want to protect it at all costs.

## Boundaries To Guard Your Temple

God desires you protect his transformative work. He does not want outside influences to disrupt his sanctifying work. Boundaries are imperative because they protect you from evil and prevent contamination from the unsanctified behaviors, beliefs, and sins of others.

Boundaries are protective barriers you erect in your spirit, soul, and body to guard against weaknesses. Think of road construction sites you pass on an interstate. Typically, guardrails or walls made of solid concrete protect these concentrated work areas. If a distracted or high-speed driver hits the wall, although the concrete and car may be damaged, the workers and equipment remain unscathed.

Establishing boundaries seems easy until you come face-to-face with temptations. Boundaries require proactive discipline on your part and taking responsibility for your actions. When faced with weaknesses you may feel your guardrails shift and self-determination crumble. In those moments, call on something more powerful—the supernatural strength of Jesus.

Jesus brings healing to and freedom from your weaknesses when you take them to the cross daily. This intentional act strengthens your boundaries and prepares you for battle, empowering you to stand strong prior to the Enemy's assault (1 John 2:16–17).

## Rivers of Living Water—Your Heavenly Treasure

Have you watched children playing in a fountain on a hot summer day? Running through the sprays of water, feeling the cool refreshment. Splashing one another and removed from life's difficulties, if only for a moment. This is a picture of God's living water flowing through and refreshing us.

It all starts in the deep well. Spirit to spirit. Allow God to fill you with his spiritual waters to flow through and refresh others, like the fountain on a hot summer day. When they experience Jesus through you, they will want more.

> "Oh, taste and see that the LORD is good! Blessed is the man who takes refuge in him!" (Psalm 34:8).

Although those Tonka truck memories are a cherished childhood treasure, God's *rivers of living water* are a heavenly treasure I protect. Proverbs 4:23 commands every follower to guard the *springs of life* (John 7:38) flowing from God's heavenly throne (Revelation 22:1) into your heart. Guard the good work the Holy Spirit is doing within you by keeping your walk with Jesus first priority.

## Action Steps

**1.** Using the analogy of the Most Holy Place, the Holy Place, and the Outer Court, write what these boundaries mean for your life, including the challenges.

**2.** Identify one action point you can engage now to guard your spirit, soul and body.

## Next Step on the Path

Do you wonder how to discover God's will for your life? Read 2 Peter 1:3–8 to prepare for the next chapter.

*Chapter Twenty-Two*

# How Can I Discover God's Will?

**God's will is not what we do—it is who we become through our relationship with him.**

The name of a local Beijing restaurant scribbled on a napkin was partially Mandarin and of no use. Far from the hostel where I was staying, I spotted two young men. I showed them the napkin and they nodded for me to follow them down an alley. Fear crept in as the alley grew dark and quiet.

At the end, they pointed to a building a block away—the restaurant. I enjoyed the exceptional Chinese cuisine, laughing to myself over my initial fear. Having visited more than forty countries as a missionary and tourist, I love to explore paths seldom traveled. You don't always find the best encounters at your destination. Sometimes, the finest stories develop along the journey.

## On the Journey Toward Our Purpose

We all are passionate about something. Some may feel as if their passion has been part of them since birth. For others, the passion may have developed later.

The purpose for our existence is to overcome what we hate or will not tolerate. We might hate poverty, spousal abuse, divorce, obesity, addictions, terrorism, child or elder neglect, or social injustices.

If left unchecked, hate can develop into sin. When hate is surrendered to God, he channels this strong emotion into a productive passion.

> "For this very reason, make every effort to supplement your faith with virtue, and virtue with knowledge, and knowledge with self-control, and self-control with stead-fastness, and steadfastness with godliness, and godliness with brotherly affection, and brotherly affection with love. For if these qualities are yours and are increasing, they keep you from being ineffective or unfruitful in the knowledge of our Lord Jesus Christ" (2 Peter 1:5–8).

## How to Know God's Will

"How can I know God's will?" is a question most Christ-followers ask. I sought an answer for years. One truth became clear, *God's will for your life is not what you do—it is who you become through your relationship with him.*

One tool serves as a road map to knowing God's will, the "How to Know God's Will" chart, given to me by my friend, Sam McMillian, founder of His High Places[5] in West Jefferson, NC. I wanted to know God's leading in life, career, relationships, and service, and this

---

[5] His High Places is a flourishing counseling ministry in West Jefferson, NC. Should you find yourself in a crisis or crossroads, consider a five-day intensive counseling and mentoring program just as I did. Website: hishighplaces.org.

chart confirmed God's desires for me. A sample of the chart—which eventually led to writing this book—is shown below. I have also included a blank sample for you to complete. To request additional copies, go to scottschuler.org/contact.

Start using this tool by writing a specific, answerable question regarding your future. My question to God in 2013 was "God, what is your will for my life and what direction do you desire me to pursue next?" Be direct both in your question and in your pursuit of a specific answer from God.

Over the next weeks, record notes and thoughts within each category on the chart. Do not complete the chart in one sitting. Add to it as you sense God speaking to you through circumstances, other people, and your personal Bible study and prayer time.

Each category of the "How to Know God's Will" chart has a distinct meaning and purpose. Scriptures are listed in each category heading. Read and ponder these verses. God will help you understand the scriptural importance of the category.

1. **Scripture and Text**. In this category, list verses from Bible studies, devotions, or conversations. A Scripture may *stop you in your tracks* because it applies in the moment. Do not overthink this step. Simply write the verses on your chart. (Read 2 Timothy 3:15–17 and Jeremiah 33:3 for biblical support of this category.)

2. **Circumstances**. With God, there are no coincidences. God works in all things at all times. List situations from your past or present circumstances that may help you flesh out how God spoke through daily events. (Read Ecclesiastes 3 and Luke 2:8–20 for biblical support of this category.)

3. **People, Actions, and Words.** God speaks through the words and actions of others. Record what people say to you in person, social media, emails, or text messages. Include gestures

relevant to the question you asked God. Write details and words God brings to your attention. The emerging patterns God communicates through the actions and words of others will amaze you. (Read Acts 9:10–19 for biblical support of this category.)

4. **Words from the Holy Spirit, Visions, Dreams, and Prophecies.** As a follower of Jesus, the Holy Spirit lives within you. The Spirit may prompt you through words, visions, dreams, and prophecies about your circumstances. Make note of these events, especially when you see them repeatedly. They may seem ordinary and insignificant, but God will help you see the extraordinary picture he is painting. (Read John 16:7–8 for biblical support of this category.)

5. **Conscience—the Peace of God.** Your conscience is inner insight guiding your values and ability to discern right from wrong. When you experience the peace of God in your conscience, you are freed from external disturbances, and your mind rests. Take notes about peaceful experiences. (Read Philippians 4:6–7 for biblical support of this category.)

6. **Heart's Desire.** Do you have a dream or a legacy you'd like to leave? Even if it seems farfetched, write it on the chart. Dream big. Express your heart's desires to God. (Read Psalm 37:4 for biblical support of this category.)

7. **Unusual display of God's humor.** This category is fun because your imagination can roam. God speaks through humorous situations, such as the *Be Holy* license plates Lory and I saw when we were engaged. These incidents may seem odd at the time but do not chalk them up to coincidence because God will use humor to speak to your heart. (Read Matthew 7:3 for biblical support of this category.)

Following is an example excerpted from my own chart, which I created over a two-year period.

## How to Know God's Will Chart

The direct, answerable question I am asking God is:

**"God, what is your will for my life and what direction do you desire me to pursue next?"**

| Scripture | Circumstances | People, Actions & Words | Words from the Holy Spirit, Visions, Dreams, Prophecies | Conscience: The Peace of God | Heart's Desire | Unusual Displays of God's Humor |
|---|---|---|---|---|---|---|
| 2 Timothy 3:15–17<br><br>Jeremiah 33:3 | Ecclesiastics 3<br><br>Luke 2:8–20 | Acts 9:10–19 | John 16:7–8 | Philippians 4:6–7 | Psalm 37:4 | Matthew 7:3 |
| 1 Peter 5:10 "And the God of all grace, who called you to his eternal glory in Christ, after you have suffered a little while, will himself restore you and make you strong, firm and steadfast." | I read this text in a Boston church in 2001: Psalm 51:10–13<br><br>"Create in me a pure heart …Restore to me the joy of your salvation … Then I will teach transgressors your ways…" | Ben said: "Thank you for being the teacher you are … God is working through you to prepare disciples for the work God has chosen for them. It's a gift and calling from God that you have." | God spoke: "You will write a book and it will be widely read."<br><br>Son, be resolved doing all things for the gospel of Jesus and spreading it. | Every time I asked God for a sign or something about the future … he delivered w/o fail.<br><br>The sign seemed to repeat the message about being a teacher of his Word. | Prayed over and over that God would restore my heart to get me ready to teach to fill that deep desire to serve him and others. | Many times, I questioned the impact I've had teaching others about Jesus. W/o fail God sent me a message from someone as if to say … "Are you kidding me …" |

| Scripture | Circumstances | People, Actions & Words | Words from the Holy Spirit, Visions, Dreams, Prophecies | Conscience: The Peace of God | Heart's Desire | Unusual Displays of God's Humor |
|---|---|---|---|---|---|---|
| 2 Timothy 3:15–17<br>Jeremiah 33:3 | Ecclesiastes 3<br>Luke 2:8–20 | Acts 9:10–19 | John 16:7–8 | Philippians 4:6–7 | Psalm 37:4 | Matthew 7:3 |
| | | | | | | |

As you begin your "How to Know God's Will" chart, remember this process is not a race to receive God's answer to the question. It is a journey—so enjoy the trip. As you make entries on the chart, God will speak through these categories and eventually answer your question by revealing and confirming a pattern.

In my chart, which eventually filled six legal-sized pages, I highlighted a common theme God revealed as the answer to my question. "Teach" was God's overall message to me. He clarified he wants me to teach others how to navigate their journey with Jesus, sharing with others what he has taught me. After six years of searching and seeking God's desire, the completion of this book results from revelation through my "How to Know God's Will" chart. As the psalmist affirms, "Delight yourself in the LORD, and he will give you the desires of your heart" (Psalm 37:4).

Take *delight* and celebrate through all Jesus will do to reveal himself to you through the chart. Stay grounded in your faith and enjoy the journey. Keep your eyes on him and not your presumed destination. Recognize and praise God for the victories he gives you in the present moments. They are new beginnings, for he is the one who promises, "Behold, I am making all things new" (Revelation 21:5).

## A Journey Along a Narrow Path

Lory and I continue to trek through new places as we embrace our love for Jesus and each other. During one excursion, we hiked a trail in the NC mountains with a specific purpose in mind—to celebrate communion with Jesus and express gratitude for our marriage, family, and the innumerable blessings he has given us. We approached a fork in the path—one direction was an easy, wide trail filled with people. The other was a rocky, steep climb with no other hikers in sight. I thought about Matthew 7:13–14, the wide path leading to destruction and the narrow path leading to life. Guess which path we took?

After hiking for a while alongside a rushing stream, bubbling over branches and rocks, we stopped to celebrate communion with prayer, bread, and juice. We found the perfect spot atop a rock in center of the stream. The sunlight bounced off the rushing water, the coolness contrasting the sun's warmth. The presence of Jesus was tangible.

As we continued our journey along the narrow path, we crested a hill and encountered a deer then a wild turkey. Because we had chosen the less traveled path, we witnessed the beauty of God's creation undisturbed. Eventually our journey led us back to the starting point—the fork in the road, filled with people, some whining about the spider webs and humidity instead of embracing and celebrating their journey.

Whether you are walking through a dark, narrow alley in Beijing or hiking a steep, rocky mountain path, learning to celebrate the richness of Jesus in the present moment is a choice. It can release you from the worries of tomorrow and the pain of the past. Lory and I walk with Jesus in joy and love; we pray you will experience his joy and love too.

## Walking with Jesus

As we close this part of our journey together, remember these principles:

- ➤ Your walk with Jesus is a lifelong pursuit—a marathon, not a sprint.
- ➤ The more you learn, the more God expects of you. Your responsibility is to walk the narrow path. Guard the good work God is doing.
- ➤ As you grow closer to Jesus, be faithful in applying this book's tools in your daily walk. Revisit the chapters regularly.

Thanks for taking this journey with me. My prayer is you have a better understanding of who God is and how the Enemy works against you. I hope you have developed a deeper relationship with your Savior, Jesus as you've grown to understand who you are, a child of God.

## Action Steps

**1.** Using what you've learned in this book, complete your "How to Know God's Will Chart." Remember this will take time.

**2.** Take action on what God reveals through the chart. Pray specifically. Dream big and get prepared. Wait on God to open the doors to his will, in his timing.

## Next Step On the Path

Your faith walk is not just a quest to understand, embrace, and celebrate your journey. It's an opportunity to share with others what Jesus has given you. This is the Great Commission. Journal the encounters you have with Jesus. And approach life experiences as new beginnings to help you and others get this Jesus thing right.

# Acknowledgments

When a first-time author has the privilege of reflecting on who to thank for their contribution to his book, it is a surreal feeling. Someone please pinch me because here I go.

It was not my idea to write, but God's. In October 2016 his heavy hand laid upon me daily until I started writing. And writing. And writing. Five years and several revisions later, God's vision for the book is in your hands.

God warned me this journey was going to be hard (Matthew 7:14). Not sure I listened because I had no idea it was going to be this difficult. But through the course of leaning into his guidance, he continued his sanctifying work in me. I am most grateful because this manuscript is the result of what Jesus has done in me. He deserves the first thank you.

Lory, my precious wife, read every word—several times. As she edited, questioned and encouraged, she kept my feet on the ground through the journey. Without Lory, this book would not exist. Oh, and God changed her life through the writing process, too. I love you to the moon.

Our amazing kids, Matthew and Allyson, thank you for sharing me and mom with this project. I know we spent a lot of time on the book. You never complained, only encouraged. I love you both.

Speaking of complaining, a shout out to our cat, Zoey. She constantly complains when her bowl is empty, but rarely left my side as I wrote and re-wrote every word of this manuscript.

Charlie Schuler, you rock. During my lowest point in life, you knew God would bring his work to fruition, even when I challenged you. Thank you for your perseverance, Dad, and for never giving up on me.

Marianne, you are an angel disguised as a human. Some refer to you as my stepmom, but I see you as flesh and blood. You encouraged me to press through to completion. I know you have always been my biggest fan.

My in-laws, Steve and Lorraine, read every page of the initial manuscript. Thank you for being there for me, sharing your feedback and wisdom. And for supporting me and Lory the entire way.

To my dear friend, Sam. I miss you. Sam was my friend, mentor, and confidant. He passed away September 2021. His legacy lives on through his joyful heart, great wisdom, and extraordinary gift of mercy. Sam, and his wife Anita, founded His High Places counseling ministry in the mountains of North Carolina.

Bill Finley, you believed in me and saw something others chose not to. Appointing me as an elder in the church is one of my most honoring experiences. Thank you for being a great friend.

Bob Hostetler sat with Lory and me during a writer's conference. I thought my book was ready for publication. Bob knew better and suggested a beta readers' group. He was spot on with his coaching.

To our Beta Group: Steve, Brittany, Bill, Latoya, Mike, Katie, Cullen, Jeanine, Wally, Deenie, Dave, and Chris. We are grateful for your commitment to reading this book and providing exceptional feedback. You helped us get the book to its final form.

Eddie Jones, you are one crazy guy. I adore you, humor and all. Thank you for your willingness to meet even when I did not have a book. You saw the eternal impact of this book when I was still trying to figure out the next chapter. "Twenty-percenters," you said in our first meeting. "This book is for the twenty percent of the Church who is going to do something for God's Kingdom." I believe you were speaking prophetically.

Denise Loock, your editing and listening skills are exceptional. Thank you for patiently editing my book, twice. And for gracefully walking with Lory and me through the doors of the publishing world.

I had never stepped foot onto the social media field until I met my coach, Edie Melson, guru of all things social media. Thank you for digging my heels out of the dirt and helping me turn my opposition into a vision of the good in social media. Your expertise will help this book make an impact across the world.

Rhonda Rhea, you are one funny person. Even during our 7 AM coaching calls (that's 6 AM your time). We needed THE title to turn heads and captivate minds. Thank you for helping us find our WHY (see what I did there?).

Lory and I attended the Blue Ridge Mountains Christian Writers Conference and "coincidentally" picked a seat at dinner with a lovely couple who effortlessly drew us into conversation and laughter. As we were leaving the table, we asked their names. George and Karen Porter. When you read this book, you will note coincidence does not exist in the Hebrew language. Only God-incidences. Our dinner conversation began a friendship and working relationship with two people who view the publishing world differently. They have a heart for Jesus and a passion to inspire and encourage new authors. George and Karen, thank you for believing in this project and for helping us craft the manuscript into a book that will change lives.

Thank you to Bold Vision Books' team of editors and artists who worked through every detail. Amber Weigand-Buckley, you nailed the cover on your first shot! Thank you.

And to those who read this book. My prayer is for you to come to know Jesus in personal ways you never imagined. You will become the remnant Church Eddie Jones prophesied, the twenty-percenters who will make a difference in this world for God's glory.

# About Scott Schuler

Ten years into Scott's walk as a believer, he was a miserable Christian. He felt like a fake. He says, "I wasn't sure what I was looking for and tired of striving for perfection, trying to follow all the rules and be religious. I knew there was more to life, but it was out of my grasp."

Scott searched for answers through countless books. He was looking for a simple companion to the Bible to help him grow in relationship with Jesus. He also believed God wanted him to share his answers with others. Those who struggled in their faith like he did. So, he journaled. A lot.

His decades-long commitment to spiritual growth led him to earn a PhD in Christian Counseling, and to complete the School of Biblical Studies in Kiev, Ukraine. He also took some time to earn an MBA and travel more than 40 countries as a tourist and missionary.

He's never found the book. So, he wrote it himself. And now you hold it in your hands.

Scott is committed to raise up dedicated followers of Jesus by teaching others what God has taught him.

Visit Scott and his amazing wife Lory on ScottSchuler.org.

Contact Scott at scott@scottschuler.org to discuss a speaking engagement at your church, or event. Or, if you have a question.

Follow Scott on Facebook @ https://www.facebook.com/scott.schuler.399, or Twitter @ https://twitter.com/scottcschuler

Made in the USA
Monee, IL
20 October 2021